Out *of the* Spin Cycle

Devotions to Lighten Your Mother Load

Jen Hatmaker

Revell

a division of Baker Publishing Group
Grand Rapids, Michigan

Published by Revell
a division of Baker Publishing Group
P.O. Box 6287, Grand Rapids, MI 49516-6287
www.revellbooks.com

Printed in the United States of America

Library of Congress Cataloging-in-Publication Data
Hatmaker, Jen.
    Out of the spin cycle : devotions to lighten your mother load / Jen Hatmaker.
        p.   cm.
    Includes bibliographical references.
    ISBN 978-0-8007-3448-0 (pbk.)
    1. Mothers—Religious life. 2. Motherhood—Religious aspects—Christianity. 3. Jesus Christ—Meditations. I. Title.
    BV4529.18.H38 2010
    242′.6431—dc22   2009054333

Published in association with the literary agency of Alive Communications, Inc., 7680 Goddard Street, Suite 200, Colorado Springs, CO 80920. www.alivecommunications.com

15   16   17   18   19   20   14   13   12   11   10   9

This book is dedicated to the remarkable company of mamas I have in my life. I've never known women who work so hard, love so deeply, and care so genuinely. I cannot imagine one day of motherhood without you next to me.

Contents

Acknowledgments 7

Prologue: A (Fairly Lame) Ode to Mothers 9

1. I'm Perfect and My Kids Never Fight 13
2. My Kids Are Headed to Therapy 17
3. An Extra Load (of Baloney) 20
4. Thrice Holy 24
5. Chick-Fil-A, Group Baths, and Other Survival Techniques 28
6. Nacho Average Bunny 31
7. Goodness Gracious 35
8. Little Hidden Surprises 39
9. Greatness, Credit, and Other Myths of Motherhood 43
10. Today Is Tomorrow's Yesterday 47
11. No-Suri 51
12. Seven Times in a Day (Of Course I'm Not Talking about Sex) 55
13. Jesus the Magic Genie 59
14. The Cannibalization of Me 64

15. First Century Camping   68

16. A Half-Filled Bag of Doritos   72

17. Tequila Sunrise   76

18. My Empty Nest Syndrome   81

19. The Santa Debacle   85

20. Skorts: It's a Skirt That Acts like Shorts!   90

21. Egg Salad Sandwich Disorder and Road Rage   94

22. My Missing Inner Saint   99

23. Garbage for Christmas   103

24. SAHM (Sleepy Anxious Hysterical Mama)   107

25. Baby Couture (Roll Eyes Here)   110

26. Mama on a Mission   114

27. Vivienne   119

28. Our Own Little Sweatshop   123

29. Upper Percentage of the Average Rank   127

30. Working Girls   131

31. Those Are the Prunes   135

32. Dogs and Discipleship   139

33. Professional Worrier   143

34. I'm Bringing Sexy Back   147

35. Mother of the Year Award   151

36. No Loving in First Grade   155

37. Do What the Voices Say   159

38. No Hands, No Jesus   163

39. Lame Lineage   168

40. Belovedness   172

Acknowledgments

So much love to my kids—Gavin, Sydney, and Caleb—and my husband, Brandon. Without you, I'd have nothing to say. Thanks for being hysterical and filling my notebook with stories. You are the family of my dreams. (But kids? Daddy and I are moving downtown when you go to college, so no one is moving home. K-thanks-bye.)

Endless gratitude to my mom, my grandmas, and my mother-in-law (who has known me almost half my life). You are my mothers. I learned everything important from you: sending a high school graduation gift to someone in her sophomore year of college can be passed off as "quirky," more butter and salt are the cure for every recipe, and it is possible to raise a "spirited" son in such a way that someone will actually want to marry him someday (nice work, Jacki).

Much appreciation to Jean Blackmer with MOPS, who fetched me for this project for reasons that are still fuzzy, but thanks. And to Andrea Doering with Revell, who simply laughed when I joined a conference call an hour late (I have a college degree but can't master time zones). Thanks for letting me be me, but also adding your sensitivity and discernment to the mix ("Dear Jen, we love this book! It's fantastic! There were just a few places we needed to tone it down. . . .").

Finally, thank you, Jesus, for being amazing and astonishing and brilliant and perfect. All the Scriptures and stories in this book are from the Gospels; our story is weaved into yours. You are wise in every way. You are the standard to which we all aspire. As mothers, teach us to love, to lead, to trust, and to obey.

Prologue

A (Fairly Lame) Ode to Mothers

An ode to the marvelous woman called "Mother"
Though not one of us is exactly like another.
From the second we're born to the minute we die
Our preferences are as limitless as stars in the sky.

We might have been perfectly gracious before
But childbirth entered us in the Mommy War.
Rather than letting everyone else be
We criticize parenting that isn't exactly like . . . me.

So once and for all let me put this to rest
None of us owns the title of "best."
Natural childbirth does not make you a hippy
Epidurals are not just for women who want to feel
    trippy.
In a bathtub with a doula or in a hospital bed
We all got a baby with limbs and a head.

Nursing is great if nothing goes wrong
But some nipples turn inward and refuse to play
    along.
This is a choice for each mom—it's *her* route
So it's just A + B and everyone else can C their way
    out.

Schedules and timers do not make you cruel
Feeding on demand does not make you a fool.
In the nursery with a monitor or in the family bed
Every chick gets to pick where her baby lays his head.

If I see one more mom roll her eyes at "organic . . ."
"Partially hydrogenated" throws some of us into
    panic.
But neither judge Sonic burgers and fries
Some of us just want to enjoy food before we die.

Preschool, home school, public, or Montessori
Listen, my friends, and I'll tell you a story:
Two moms differed on favorite school trends
Their kids turned out pretty much the same. The
    end.

If a girl gets the title of "mom" accidentally
The worst thing we can do is treat her judgmentally.
How about some love, some help, some advice?
She needs our love and we shouldn't think twice.

Discipline through various methods will prevail
Look, we're all just trying to keep our kids out of
    jail.
These things are just preferences, not right or wrong
What matters more is teaching our kids to get
    along—
To love and to share, to speak gently and kind,
To obey so that mom won't go out of her mind.

Showing them Jesus is our common ground
Teaching them how he can always be found.
He's present in public school and Waldorf (so trendy)
He's over at Whole Foods but also at Wendy's.
Jesus never cared about these sorts of things
It's our hearts that he wants and the worship we
    bring.

It's time for us moms to declare a truce
Regardless if we buy Capri Sun or 100 percent juice.
My way is not your way, and your way isn't mine
But both of our kids will turn out just fine.

Rather than judging and looking down our noses
Let's enjoy the common ground motherhood poses.
As believers, we all love the same good Lord
We all have children who tell us "I'm bored."

We all need more sleep than these tiny five hours
Most of us struggle to find time for a shower.
We haven't been to the bathroom alone in an age
Our mothers have all told us, "Relax, this is just a
     stage."

We all love our babies so much we could die
We'd take a bullet for each one without batting an
     eye.
Though we are different, we're in the same tribe
Motherhood requires a similar vibe—
Love and affection, sacrifice and grace
Laughter, which keeps the whole mechanism in place.

Though different, by the grace of God, I suspect:
ALL our children will rise up and call us . . . collect.

She looks well to how things go in her household. . . . Her
children rise up and call her blessed.

                              Proverbs 31:27–28 AMP

1

I'm Perfect and My Kids Never Fight

Everything [the Pharisees] do is done for men to see: They make their phylacteries wide and the tassels on their garments long; they love the place of honor at banquets and the most important seats in the synagogues; they love to be greeted in the marketplaces and to have men call them "Rabbi."

Matthew 23:5–7

My youngest son Caleb is what we like to call a "pistol." He is a constant challenge to harness, but his hilarious antics inspired my husband to dub him "our family mascot." Any time he talks to an adult without me there to monitor the discussion, I'm terribly nervous, and Caleb's first grade teacher has given me much ammunition to support that paranoia. Evidently, when she recently asked what they wanted to be when they grew up, Caleb raised his eager little hand and replied, "When I grow up, I want to be a missionary and tell

13

people about God, even though my mom told me all missionaries get murdered."

Note to self: When talking to my kids about the freedom to go to church whenever and however we want, exercise caution when elaborating on how *some* people in other countries can't go to church and—wait for it—even die for their faith, because the six-year-old will tweak that factoid and make me sound like a dimwit during the retelling.

Insert the sound of me babbling like an idiot to her, defending my discussion with my six-year-old while simultaneously throwing him under the bus for butchering the teaching moment I thought I was handling so beautifully. For some reason, it mattered to me that this young teacher did not think I was a psycho, lest I become the fodder for Teachers' Lounge Stories, which I think we can all safely assume I already am.

Motherhood triggers something that went dormant about the time we left middle school. We're seeded with this desire to be thought well of, to be admired, to be affirmed in our hard work as moms. We tend to report our babies as sleeping longer than they do, our discipline as working more often than it does, and our systems as creating some efficient home that doesn't exist. We are masters at propping up our lives, spinning a thread of truth into an elaborate tapestry of grandeur—when in fact, during young motherhood most of us live in what my girlfriend Loren calls a "poop storm."

I'm just saying.

Jesus understood this tendency, as the religious leaders during his day were characterized by their constant preening and posturing, presenting an image that had precious little to do with reality. What other people thought of them and how they were perceived became supreme, and they sacrificed greatly to maintain their image.

Wait, what? The *Pharisees* sacrificed? That's right. They gave up genuine relationships, first and foremost. They never operated like real humans, so no one could relate to them honestly. They created paranoia in everyone they spoke to.

Consequently, people pretended around the Pharisees as much as the Pharisees pretended around other people. They must have been the loneliest people on earth.

This principle holds true today. When we operate from the central concern of being seen a certain way, we can't develop healthy relationships in the messy soil of reality—the only place they'll grow. Presenting a perfect, fake life to others generates fear in our own hearts and intimidation in everyone else's, and creates nice, fake relationships—with our friends, with our family members, even with our own children.

The tight hold the religious leaders had on principles, theology, and image lost them their chance to become friends of Jesus, whose inner circle was made up of prostitutes, liars, cowards, and nobodies. Not only did Jesus *not* require perfection, those who pretended they'd attained it disgusted him.

Authenticity ranks terribly high on Jesus's list of required attributes. It's not how good we are that counts, but how truthful we are about how good we're not. Only then can Jesus get busy developing us into the redeemed daughters we already are in him.

Can we just let the posturing go? Can we speak truth to each other and reach out for help when we need it? Can we admit our failures and stop worrying about what someone might think? Can we allow others to be the same people on the outside as they are on the inside? Can we live real lives in front of each other, imperfect in our humanity but reclaimed through Jesus?

I will if you will.

If you and I do, others can.

If we all do, everyone might.

○ Do you have a struggle, doubt, temptation, or crisis no one knows about—big or small?

○ What is the primary reason you haven't told anyone?

STEP OUT OF THE SPIN CYCLE

Take a step toward authenticity today. With whom can you lay your pretense down and speak the truth? Call, write, or email that person today. Invite them into your life in a genuine way.

Perhaps that person is Jesus . . .

My Kids Are Headed to Therapy

My husband and I moved the same weekend we launched our new church, making us the stupidest people who have ever breathed air. Adding to the mayhem, our three kids transferred to their new school and were completing their very first week. In a sadistic twist of fate, that Friday was Field Day, where all three wanted me to cheer them on and take pictures and whatnot like the other good moms.

But because we were moving, my "time awareness" was impaired. I'd promised to bring my kindergartener lunch; I showed up fifteen minutes late to find him sitting with his head on the table, crying, while other parents tried to give him food, thinking the new kid was probably on welfare.

From that lovely scene, I ran to watch my second grader's race only to find her sitting against the wall with puffy, I've-been-bawling eyes. "She's been saying she feels sick all day.

She thought you would be here by now, and I think she's just disappointed," said her teacher, in the most nonhelpful manner in the history of time.

After some unsuccessful damage control, I sprinted to my fourth grader's sack race to discover he was the only kid who wasn't wearing a green shirt, didn't have a water bottle, and hadn't donned a headband. He took one look at me, and his face said it all.

I cried the whole way home.

Who knew parenting would be this hard? Who knew there would be ten thousand details to keep up with all day, every day? Who knew there was a mommy competition we were automatically entered into the day we gave birth? Who knew how frequently we would fail our kids? Or how much that would hurt? Who knew we'd constantly worry our kids would end up on the therapy couch?

Will I ever be enough as a mom? "It is enough for the student to be like his teacher," Jesus counseled gently (Matt. 10:25).

When the student becomes like her teacher, our failures and omissions as moms recede as the sweet spirit of Jesus covers our humanity. Our children won't remember every paper we forgot to sign, or the week we fed them hot dogs for seven straight days. They'll forget how we blew off bathtime and bribed them to watch Dora for *thirty minutes of blessed silence.*

What they will remember is how we prayed with them and listened to their little dreams and fears. They'll never forget how we cared for the broken members of our community, teaching them the mission of Jesus. So vividly will they remember how slow we were to judge, and how quick we were to laugh. Our kids will recall how wildly we loved them, beyond reason and past boundaries.

The right schools, the right clubs, the right teams . . . not enough.

Perfect systems and by-the-book methods . . . not enough.

Superior advantages and strategic positioning . . . not enough.

It is enough for me to show patience when I want to stick my fingers in my ears and scream like a toddler. It is enough to choose mercy when they've made the same mistake yet again. It is enough to imitate my Christ, who never jumped through conventional hoops but transformed the trajectory of history through grace and sacrifice.

You are *enough* as a mother when you act like your Redeemer, dear one. When you talk like he talked, love like he loved, forgive like he forgave, and teach like he taught. When you launch your children into this big, exciting, wonderful world, that is all that will matter. It is what they'll remember and imitate.

It is enough.

Mother is the name for God in the lips and hearts of little children.

William Makepeace Thackeray

○ As a mom, does the goal of becoming like your teacher feel like enough?

STEP OUT OF THE SPIN CYCLE

For the rest of the day, try to filter every word, decision, and activity with your kids through the grid of being like Jesus—and nothing else.

An Extra Load

(of Baloney)

My friend Stephanie teaches first grade at an affluent school in Austin. During the first week of classes, a concerned father (read: crazy) cornered her and asked, "What are you doing to prepare my son for Yale?" Quick on her feet and not in the mood for intimidation, Stephanie answered, "Well, first I'm going to teach him to stop picking his nose and eating the plunder. Next up is walking in a straight line for more than five seconds. I'll be ready to write a recommendation to Yale by the end of the year, I'm sure."

Why do people add so much pressure onto an already challenging task? Never is this truer than with motherhood. Early childhood is this bizarre world where we hyperventilate because another mom enrolled her four-month-old in Spanish classes, while assuring you that at eleven months, the language acquisition window has certainly closed for your baby. Sorry for your luck.

Or a woman at the park casually asks you what waiting lists you have your two-week-old on, while making it crystal clear that unless you expose her to Montessori curriculum (may also insert: Waldorf, High/Scope, Bank Street, Reggio-Emilia, Abeca, *whatever*), then you're basically reserving her a spot in "Life Skills Class" in high school. This pressure, I'm pretty sure, is why the term "It's five o'clock somewhere" was coined.

This is not a new phenomenon, nor is it restricted to the obnoxious world of motherhood, girls. In first century Judea, religious leaders—who overcomplicated the basic obedient life most tried to live—dictated Jewish culture. In addition to the law through Moses (which alone would make me consider a cocktail habit), they piled "extra teachings" on top of the billion rules the Jews already had to follow.

The religious leaders transformed the Ten Commandments into such a complex ethical system of regulations and clauses that pretty much anything but breathing was somehow offensive. For instance, the rabbis expanded the simple prohibition of certain meats into an impossible system of kosher laws that made the Jews so paranoid, I bet they ate tree bark to be safe.

All these extra teachings, additional rules, added standards, and supplementary laws were described by one term familiar to every Jew under the crushing weight of a law that simply couldn't be kept: "yoke." Each rabbi had his own unique yoke encompassing *his* interpretations and additional mandates. The rabbis' yokes were well known, and you could determine who followed whom by which extra rules someone was keeping. A rabbi's followers were expected to adhere to his yoke, complete with guilt, shame, condemnation, and failure.

Enter Jesus.

Come to me, all you who are weary and burdened, and I will give you rest. Take my yoke upon you and learn from me, for I am gentle and humble in heart, and you will find rest for your souls. For my yoke is easy and my burden is light.

Matthew 11:28–30

How meaningful those words were to the normal, exhausted, defeated Jew longing for relief. Do you see how this rabbi was so unlike his contemporaries? This is our Savior. He takes the unnecessary pressure and pointless legalism, either thrust upon us or self-imposed, and he gently pushes those aside and says, "Come to me."

There is a rest that only exists in Christ. In his embrace we can discern between what matters and what doesn't, what counts and what is simply optional, and what is essential to our holy task as mothers and what is just cultural pressure. Jesus always chooses the simple over the complicated, the humble over the elaborate.

Can you hear the spirit of his voice? He does not want moms wasting away in guilt and condemnation. He hates that you wallow in doubt and succumb to unnecessary pressure as you raise your sweet babies. Come to him. Come to his gentle ways and his humble approaches. Come to his rest and liberation. Come to that place where you don't bend to every suggestion or bow to every criticism.

Come and rest.

His yoke is easier than the one you're wearing.

○ What yoke have you put on that is wearing you out and stealing your joy?

STEP OUT OF THE SPIN CYCLE

What would you need to let go of to take on Jesus's yoke instead? What tangible step can you take to start that process of liberation today?

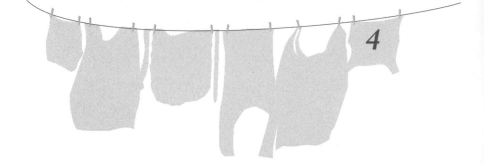

Thrice Holy

Not long ago, my sisters and I drove to Wichita, Kansas, to celebrate our dad's last day as a pastor in the church we grew up in. Think: organs, choir robes, and pantyhose (Satan's fabric). For some reason that escapes me now, we sat in the front row. Understand that my sisters and I are trouble. The only venue we should sit in the front row at is a Bon Jovi concert. One hundred pairs of Choir People eyes stared at us, basically ensuring we would somehow disgrace the family name during the service.

Enter the worship pastor, with his special hair and penchant for melodrama and rolled Rs. Reluctant to leave the spotlight, he extended his podium moment with a prayer, and so help me, this is what he said:

"Oooohhhhhh, blessed Lord of the Harvest (dramatic pause) . . . You. Are. THRICE! HOLY!"

And because I'm so mature, a Christian author and speaker no less, I burst out laughing. Shoulders shaking, tears pouring, trying-to-be-silent hysteria. My sisters were just as bad, and we entered the Can't Stop Laughing In Church Nightmare. I fixated on bad thoughts to shut off the giggle valve—*death, disease, malnutrition, humidity*—but nothing helped. As soon as one sister calmed down, another would start with the shoulder shaking, and we derailed again. The Choir Eyes were not happy, and my mom wanted to murder us. (I'd like to say we were teenagers, but we were in our thirties. Sad.)

Really? "Thrice holy"? Is that even a real phrase? I don't know if that was intended to impress God or the congregation, but I'll go to the grave saying it impressed neither. What is it with fancy praying? What is the deal with wordy phraseology and Christianese? Why is the Christian community so plagued with weird-sounding prayers fueled by rote phrases and a massive overuse of the words "Lord" and "just"? ("Lord, I just ask you, Lord . . .")

Perhaps no service rendered to our children is more important than our intercession. A mother's job is to pray for her children while they don't have the words, understanding, or insight to pray for themselves. We stand in the gap, praying for their salvation, gifts, and lives, much like the Spirit prays for us.

What matters when we pray is not the lovely (or weird) words we use. It doesn't matter if the prayer sounds pretty, if it flows right, if it's in some perfect order, or if it was long enough. You don't need to be an accomplished public pray-er or fluent in Christian lingo. In fact, Jesus doesn't even like that stuff. Here is how he put it:

> When you pray, do not keep on babbling like the pagans, for they think they will be heard because of their many words. Do not be like them, for your Father knows what you need before you ask him.
>
> Matthew 6:7–8

25

It doesn't matter how we say it, but *that* we say it: "God, draw my children to you early and urgently." The words you choose are inconsequential, but it is essential that you pray, "Holy Spirit, lead my son every second of his life." It doesn't matter if we're on our knees or in our car when we ask, "Jesus, show my children to love the way you loved."

Sometimes we don't even know what to ask for; we just desperately want God's intervention in the lives of our children. Here is some good news:

> The Holy Spirit helps us in our weakness. For example, we don't know what God wants us to pray for. But the Holy Spirit prays for us with groanings that cannot be expressed in words. And the Father who knows all hearts knows what the Spirit is saying, for the Spirit pleads for us believers in harmony with God's own will.
>
> Romans 8:26–27 NLT

> [Jesus] is able to save completely those who come to God through him, because he always lives to intercede for them.
>
> Hebrews 7:25

Be comforted, young mom. Between you, Jesus, and the Holy Spirit, your children are being well prayed for—even perfectly prayed for. Your prayers may be rudimentary, but Jesus lives to intercede for your babies; the Spirit pleads in harmony with God's own will for them, a will that includes salvation, strength, healthy relationships, security in Jesus, their mission, their giftedness, their purpose—all the things you want most for them. You are not alone in your prayers.

You + Jesus + the Spirit . . .

Now *that* is thrice wonderful.

○ How do you feel about praying?

○ If you could completely set aside any hang-ups about "praying well," would you intercede for your children more often?

STEP OUT OF THE SPIN CYCLE

What is the most pressing need you can intercede for today? Go there.

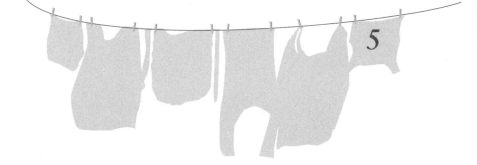

5

Chick-Fil-A, Group Baths, and Other Survival Techniques

I'm a terrible driver when I'm alone. It always seems like a great idea at first. I relish the notion of being in the car without the following verbal barrage assaulting me like tiny, individual daggers stabbing away at the thin flesh of my sanity:

"Mommy? Do you know how to teleport?"

"Mommy? How many seconds have you been alive?"

"Mommy? What's five billion times ten million?"

"Mommy? When I go to college, will you be dead?"

But the reality of driving alone is much different than the beautiful, peaceful theory. I get bored. I get tired. With my arm on the steering wheel, I start noticing how loose the flesh under my arm is. It hangs like a slab of beef. I obsess about this slab by repeatedly pinching it with my free hand. I promise the slab I will take it to the gym and attempt to eradicate it. I drift off the shoulder of the road, which scares me into attentiveness for at least four minutes. I flip through the radio stations and discover I don't know who is popular anymore—and *I was cool just a few years ago*. Land sakes! Am I there yet?

I should have brought a friend.

Traveling alone just doesn't compare to traveling with friends. Friends help you uphold the heavy responsibility of motherhood and remind you you're not crazy. They don't complain when your kids interrupt your phone conversation every twelve seconds. They gladly enter the parenting discussions that our husbands lose patience with after only the fourth time. Friends don't even bat an eye when you burst out crying *for no good reason*.

The way we love each other, serve each other, and live our lives with each other is a big deal to Jesus. At the beginning of time, creation encountered its first problem: "It is not good for the man to be alone." Thus history began with human connection. Two are better than one, and togetherness is always superior to loneliness.

Never was I more susceptible to isolation than during young motherhood. It can be such lonely work. Because my personality required a scheduled routine, for years I fed and dressed babies→cleaned up→put someone down for a morning nap→engineered lunch chaos→put kids down for afternoon naps→cooked dinner→bath time→story time→bedtime. I'd sit down for the first time at 8 p.m.

It was *hard* to make room for my friends. But I did it. We had playdates down to a science. We put babies to sleep at each other's houses, bathed them together, fed them together, ate at Chick-Fil-A so often the manager knew us by name, and picnicked at every park in the greater Austin area. I changed their babies' diapers as often as mine. We put each other's kids in time-out. I administered first aid to their children, and they pulled mine out of the swimming pool. We've traded kids, taken kids, borrowed kids, and dumped kids.

My friends are the reason I survived young motherhood.

> A new command I give you: Love one another. As I have loved you, so you must love one another. By this all men will know that you are my disciples, if you love one another.
>
> John 13:34–35

If we are to love each other like Jesus loved us, then it makes practical sense to band together during young motherhood. Because—like Jesus does—we'll end up loving each other when we're crazy, burned out, hysterical, and exhausted. We'll stand by one another during the most neurotic phase of parenting there is. We won't let a member of our tribe slip under the radar or get swallowed by isolation. We share the burden of parenting, making it lighter for everyone to carry. We'll remind our friends to laugh and call forward the best in each other.

Motherhood is the task that brings us together, but love is the glue that binds us together. If we're too busy to love each other like this, then we're too busy. We need our friends. We need their counsel and companionship; they need our compassion and comic relief.

"You *must* love one another," said Jesus.

We really must.

○ Are you enjoying the tribe of young mothers, or are you lonely and isolated? Why?

STEP OUT OF THE SPIN CYCLE

Reach out to another mom or group of moms today. Invite them over, plan a playdate, arrange a picnic, whatever. Need a friend? Be a friend.

6

Nacho Average Bunny

Brandon and I started a church called Austin New Church, whose mantra is "Love your neighbor. Serve your city." One branch of the church is on the east side of Austin, a low-income, mostly Latino section of town. Together, we offered Vacation Bible School for their community.

Perhaps no living being is less into children's ministry than me, but drop it on the east side with a bunch of shirtless, adorable, mocha-skinned kids, and I'll invent some reason to be there. Terrible at this sort of thing, I was loosely assigned as a "craft helper," with no discernible responsibilities and thus less of a risk for tanking a rotation.

As I admired the kids' art, I noticed Carlos—about seven—drawing an impressive bunny. (The bunny had nothing to do with the day's lesson, which was the story of Jesus walking on water, but art is subjective, no?) I leaned in closer and, prodding for clarity, said:

"Great work, Carlos! Hey, what's in the bunny's hand?"

And without looking up, with no emotion or further explanation, Carlos replied:

"A knife."

Alrighty then. And why wouldn't an innocent bunny be wielding a knife? Shouldn't they all? You've got to stay sharp when you're all cute and fluffy, since you're basically inviting an attack. You might think that a bunny is a soft target, an easy hit, but you'd be wrong; Carlos's bunny will cut you.

Carlos's knife-wielding baby rabbit comes to mind when I read about Jesus commissioning his disciples out into the world:

> I am sending you out like sheep among wolves. Therefore be as shrewd as snakes and as innocent as doves.
>
> Matthew 10:16

"Shrewd" in the original Greek means "wise, prudent." It includes keenness, constant awareness, discernment, the ability to say the right thing at the right time and to consider context, and sharp common sense. It's the opposite of clueless. It's the mom who sizes up a situation and watches for social cues and red flags. It's the mom who follows her instincts and refuses to ignore a gut check. It's the mom who realizes she is parenting in an ever-changing world full of landmines and trapdoors. Shrewd parenting is ever diligent, never allowing apathy or naïveté to blind us while the enemy claims our children.

But many moms take the second half of this complicated statement—"be as innocent as doves"—and decide to avoid the landmines, raise their children in innocence, and "be shrewd" by simply sequestering them from the world. If we create a utopian environment, bubble-wrapped in Christian subculture, then perhaps our kids will emerge as Jesus Juniors.

This position gets wrecked when we look at the context of Jesus's statement: "I am sending you out." This is not a gray area. This isn't complicated. He was simply advising us on how to conduct ourselves as we obey the given that we are a *sent people*, not people meant to sequester ourselves with other Christians and avoid culture as much as possible.

Jesus knows that Christians will exist in an impure environment. He would never favor a moral purity that avoids contact with the impurities of the world. Jesus lived in the marketplace. He partied with known sinners. He went to their houses and had meals with them. His reputation among the moral purists of his day was a "glutton, drunkard and a friend of sinners" (Matt. 11:16).

He sends us out shrewdly innocent. But innocent here doesn't mean what you might think. It is not an umbrella term encompassing all our "do nots"—as in Christians do not _____ (or have any fun). Innocent literally means "inoffensive." See, Jesus sent us into this broken world not to defend him, but to represent him. We are to talk to those he talked to, say the kinds of things he said, and love those he loved—without polluting our message with judgment and offensiveness. We have missed the point if our worldview involves fighting *against* culture as our enemy; we imitate our Savior when we fight *for* culture as loved people yet to know their Creator.

Otherwise, why would Jesus tell us to be shrewd? If navigating this life involved Christian detachment from the rest of the world, we'd never need that skill. We'd be "safe," disengaged from the scary, bad, evil people of the world. However, Jesus sees these people as broken, lonely, desperate, and hungry for a Savior.

We do our children a tragic disservice to raise them in seclusion, falsely detaching them from the world they've been sent to help redeem. What kind of disciples are we making when our children enter the real world as shocked and clueless young adults, ill-equipped to connect with the spiritually disoriented and unable to make sense of their environment? In an effort to protect their innocence, we send them out naïve and unprepared: bunnies without knives, vulnerable and defenseless.

Your kids should be praying regularly for the kids in their school and neighborhood.

They should learn to befriend the loner, the loser, the lost.

They need to hear from you: "We don't judge. We love."

Be the happy home where people apart from God feel welcomed.

They will learn innocent shrewdness—or not—from you. It is not your responsibility to raise perfect prototypes of holiness, fit to set on a pedestal and admire. Your job is to send your children into this world as disciples who understand their mission and who will contend for God's glory.

○ Do your kids ever see you loving the lost, the poor, the spiritually disconnected?

STEP OUT OF THE SPIN CYCLE

Invite another mom who doesn't know the Lord over with her kids, or invite her and her family to go to church. Your entire goal is to love her. Represent Jesus well.

Goodness Gracious

Scanning my bookshelves, I see about a billion books on parenting. I read eight books on babies before I ever gave birth to one. I've taken Lamaze classes, BabyWise classes (don't start), and parenting classes. I've joined discussion groups on raising tweens and facilitated book studies on balanced motherhood. I've downloaded helpful sermons and read countless websites. I've made lists and plans on how to manage summer/chores/homework/discipline/sleepovers/house rules.

And then there is real motherhood, which knocks out half of this stuff.

Because sometimes, despite your careful strategizing and planning and reading and organizing, your two-year-old takes his diaper off in the middle of Target and runs up the cereal aisle while you scream at him like a mental patient. And sometimes, after you've planned the perfect playdate, your daughter bites your new friend's baby and flushes her phone down the toilet.

And sometimes, when your precious firstborn son—the one you read all the baby books for and raised lovingly for ten years—opens a fresh, sassy mouth to you when you are already idling high, you accidentally tell him to get a shovel, go in the backyard, and dig his own grave. This, I don't have to tell you, is behavior Ted Tripp would frown upon in *Shepherding a Child's Heart*.

Not surprisingly, when I made that shockingly horrible statement to my son, I was exhausted, stretched thin, out of the Word, and in a prayer slump. I was running on spiritual fumes. My only intake was whiny children, mountains of laundry, a *Suite Life of Zack & Cody* marathon, and four hundred thousand pieces of correspondence from Elm Grove Elementary to attend to.

There is a simple explanation according to Jesus:

> For out of the overflow of the heart the mouth speaks. The good man brings good things out of the good stored up in him, and the evil man brings evil things out of the evil stored up in him.
>
> Matthew 12:34–35

Motherhood is like a pitcher with a hole in the bottom: a constant drain on our energy, patience, and tolerance. Every mother who is telling the truth would attest to that. Add something like a child with autism, single motherhood, a financial crisis, or a crumbling marriage, and it's a wonder we have anything left to give.

Our only hope to speak with kindness, to lead with patience, and to not threaten our children with homicide is to ensure our spiritual reserves are not bone-dry. Moms are the middle of the flow chart; the arrows of exertion flow constantly out from us, but when no arrows of strength, grace, and peace are flowing in, the whole mechanism is in danger.

Goodness in equals goodness out.

No goodness in equals no goodness out.

This is a simple truth, recognized by Jesus and every other parenting expert, but one most moms fail to take seriously. We're too busy for the Word. We're too tired to pray. We have too much going on to join a small group. Under the banner of selflessness, we neglect our own spiritual health and sabotage the very service we want to render.

When God's Word is flowing through my life, my baby can spill his fourth drink of the day and I can say, "It's just a drink." When I'm spiritually dry, I could literally lie on the soggy floor and bawl over it. When Jesus has spoken peace into my life, I'm able to discipline consistently when my toddler pitches her third tantrum of the morning. If my pitcher is empty, I might lock myself in the bathroom and scream at the top of my lungs.

Out of the overflow of the heart the mouth speaks.

If nothing good is stored up, where are we possibly going to draw patience? Grace? Longsuffering? Young motherhood is too demanding to attempt without a deep connection to Christ. I literally don't know how women do it without him.

No, you don't have to spend an hour a day in the Word.

No, it's not necessary to look up Greek definitions and create outlines.

No, you don't need to build a prayer shrine with candles and worship music.

But a simple space at the beginning of your day before anyone needs to be attended to in any way, a moment just for you and God and his beautiful Word—this is essential. This is where goodness is stored up for the day, and you'll need it; it's perishable. This is when Jesus reminds you, "You can do this. I'm right here." It's how you become centered and remember that spilled drinks and tantrums are a blip on the timeline of your life. It's when God can whisper, "I have all you need."

Goodness in, goodness out.
Take care of the first and the second is covered.

○ How are you doing on "goodness in"?

○ Do you see a link between your answer and the words coming out of your mouth on a daily basis?

STEP OUT OF THE SPIN CYCLE

Set your alarm 15–20 minutes before your normal day begins tomorrow. Spend that time in a psalm (or whatever Scripture you want) and then in quiet prayer. Goodness in, mama.

8

Little Hidden Surprises

My husband and I are determined to raise children who aren't a drain on society or a thorn in Jesus's flesh. I don't want to sit across from my future daughter- or son-in-law and say, "I'm sorry."

My only chance at this pipe dream is to raise kids who love Jesus and are passionate about his kingdom. Only he can ensure no one is sleeping on my couch at age twenty-nine because "things just didn't work out." Any sense of purpose or mission is going to come from their relationship with God.

Jesus delivered some profound teaching in Matthew 13 on "the kingdom of heaven"—good news for every mom trying to instill that kingdom in her children:

- "The kingdom of heaven is like a man who sowed good seed in his field" (v. 24).

- "The kingdom of heaven is like a mustard seed, which a man took and planted in his field. Though it is the smallest of all your seeds, yet when it grows, it is the largest of garden plants and becomes a tree" (vv. 31–32).
- "The kingdom of heaven is like yeast that a woman took and mixed into a large amount of flour until it worked all through the dough" (v. 33).
- "The kingdom of heaven is like treasure hidden in a field" (v. 44).
- "The kingdom of heaven is like a merchant looking for fine pearls" (v. 45).
- "The kingdom of heaven is like a net that was let down into the lake and caught all kinds of fish" (v. 47).

The kingdom is like a tiny seed, yeast, hidden treasure, pearls shut up in a shell, fish under the water.

All small.

Implanting the kingdom of heaven is a series of infinitesimal teaching moments and modeling opportunities. It's the littlest instant when you show your child how to share (again), lacing kingdom words into your instruction. It's the twenty seconds you and your little one pray for the kid who hurt her feelings; a living demonstration of the kingdom principle, "Love your enemies, and pray for those who persecute you." It's the small kernel of kindness your children learn when they watch you love your neighbor or serve the forgotten.

Discipleship is never encapsulated in a moment, a weekend, a workbook. It isn't one huge event when everything locks into place and salvation is sealed. It's contained in the smallest increments, instilled over minutes, days, years. The kingdom is like a tiny seed, yeast, hidden treasure, pearls shut up in a shell, fish under the water.

All hidden . . . at first.

Who can see a seed under the soil or invisible yeast in dough? The hidden treasure is indiscernible and the pearl is locked in its casing; the fish swim invisibly under the water. Is this not also true of the kingdom we're tucking away in our children? We know godliness has been deposited, but we can't always see it on the surface.

Despite my obsession with raising kingdom-minded children, our spiritual mentorship has been met with statements including, but not limited to, the following:

- "I don't want to give my money to God! I want to be richer than God!" (Gavin, age five, on tithing).
- "I love God on Sundays and Tuesdays" (Sydney, age four, on selective devotion).
- "Dear God, please stop making barbecue sauce. It burns my tongue" (Caleb, age four, on praying).
- "Instead of being in a family that has to 'learn to make good choices' [finger quotes included], I wish I was homeless!" (Caleb, age six, on morals and career choices).

If I didn't have Jesus's teachings, these results would be quite discouraging. I have spent so many hours teaching, modeling, discipling my kids with only invisible results or hidden effects. Motherhood is often an exercise in delayed gratification. The kingdom is like a tiny seed, yeast, hidden treasure, pearls shut up in a shell, fish under the water. *Each involve surprise.*

There are a surprising variety of harvests, a surprising potential for growth, a surprising transformation of dough, a surprising treasure discovered. This is something like picking my son up from a sleepover and hearing, "We love Gavin! He has the best manners!" (Seriously?) It's the lovely surprise of tucking my daughter into bed and hearing, "Mama? I think we should adopt an orphan. We have so much love to share." It is the sweet startle of hearing from my youngest son's teacher, "Caleb is so kind to the little loner in our class."

The kingdom of heaven embedded in our children is small, hidden early, and surprisingly revealed later. All the little moments count, mama. Every small piece of wisdom you offer matters, even if its results are invisible for a while. Each tiny lesson implants a treasure in your child, exposed in time.

It might feel like small work.

You might not see a single thing working.

But you'll be surprised.

○ What kingdom principle are you planting in your children right now that you don't see the fruits of yet?

STEP OUT OF THE SPIN CYCLE

Take a small moment to seed your children with a spiritual treasure today. Think of their most common struggle, and create a teaching moment to share.

Greatness, Credit,
and Other Myths of Motherhood

I am one parenting stage ahead of most of you, dear hearts. I'm past naptimes, Boudreaux's Butt Paste, and preschool waiting lists ("Please, please, please, please . . . someone get kicked out for biting!"). But the constant need-meeting, the incessant talking, the relentless managing all comes back to me—every summer.

Here's a slice of my life yesterday (add to the kid equation my three plus four or five extra neighbor kids at all times, every day, starting at 8:30 a.m.): Can you tie my bow? Will you make me a smoothie? Caleb keeps pressing pause! I have nothing to do. I'm bleeding! Can I watch Weird Al on YouTube? Gavin locked me in the bathroom! I'm starving, Mom! We're all starving, Mrs. Hatmaker! Will you change these batteries? Sydney won't get out of my room! Where's the flashlight? How old do I have to be to legally change my name? No other kids have to do chores! I don't like to read anymore. When's lunch? Watch, Mom! Are you watching?

Moooooooooooooooooooooom!!

Mom?

Mama?

I have not had an uninterrupted thought in twelve straight days. I am in the kitchen morning, noon, and night feeding all the children of Garlic Creek. By 9:45 a.m., I've already broken up three fights. When I refused to make a third round of smoothies, Caleb replied, "This is the worst day of my life." So when hubs got home at 5:30 and said, "You seem a little tense," I seriously considered getting in *his* car (because it doesn't appear as if an army of filthy badgers live in it) and driving to Canada.

If there is a more thankless, unglamorous job than motherhood, I haven't seen it. I know you get it, girls. Something about being covered in other people's urine and vomit while scrubbing toilets and hearing your precious cherub say "NO!" to you twelve hundred times a day makes moms bat-poop-crazy sometimes. On super bad days, you might even say, "Is this really my life?" Some of you were in a boardroom or office just a couple of years ago, talking grown-up talk and wearing clean clothes. Motherhood comes with no status, no paycheck, no recognition, and very little credit.

> When [Jesus] was in the house, he asked them, "What were you arguing about on the road?" But they kept quiet because on the way they had argued about who was the greatest. [Busted.]
>
> Sitting down, Jesus called the Twelve and said, "If anyone wants to be the first, he must be the very last, and the servant of all."
>
> Mark 9:33–35

When I became a mom, "servanthood" took on a whole new meaning. In our family, we decided I would be the one to change my daily life and stay at home with the babies. But when I took that as my identity, I developed a sense of entitlement and did a lot of waiting around for credit. I held the emotional position that I was doing everyone a favor. This top-down perspective tainted everything, because if I wasn't perfectly appreciated, adequately recognized, or verbally praised (and what mom is?), then I became the wounded martyr who was always disgruntled.

Jesus transformed my idea of "being the greatest." It's not about receiving credit or being popular. It has nothing to do with position or power or getting our just due. Greatness does not come from recognition or the praises of others.

True greatness comes to us through the back door of servanthood.

As mothers, this requires an emotional shift. We are not doing our husbands and children a favor. We are intentional servants, consciously deferring to the needs of those God entrusted to us. We make the near-constant decision to cast off selfishness and resist entitlement. We deliberately choose "servant" with all our faculties in place, exactly as Jesus did in all his strength and glory.

We are not subservient doormats; that is something entirely different. Subservience means your family expects you to do what they could rightly do for themselves—you are like hired help, failing to teach your family respect and independence. I've seen many subservient moms allow their children to bark orders at them while their husbands sit in the Barca Lounger abdicating their role as the other parent. That is not healthy or godly, so don't imagine that's what Jesus meant by "servant of all."

With his knack for perfect illustrations, Jesus elaborated like this:

> He took a little child and had him stand among them. Taking him in his arms, he said to them, "Whoever welcomes one of these little children in my name welcomes me; and

whoever welcomes me does not welcome me but the one who sent me."

Mark 9:36–37

When I choose *servant* instead of *martyr*, my children enjoy the security that they are welcomed in our home. They are not a thorn in my flesh, cutting into my personal time. They aren't a nuisance, making me sigh with irritation all day. They are welcomed members of this family, loved and purposed. And when my children are welcomed, I have opened the very doors of heaven and invited God himself into the laughter, chaos, and life of our home.

Now that is greatness.

○ Do you struggle with not being appreciated? If so, how is that frustration affecting your marriage? Your parenting?

STEP OUT OF THE SPIN CYCLE

Approach today with this perspective: "I am happy to serve my family with no expectations of recognition." Choose a moment to tell your kids or husband, "I'm so glad to do this for you."

Today Is Tomorrow's Yesterday

Perhaps in the history of time, there has been nothing as unhelpful as this statement made to every mom of young children by every mom with grown children:

"Enjoy it! This will be over before you know it!"

This is usually uttered after the young mom has let a complaint leak out, something horribly self-centered like, "I'm sorry I smell like vomit. I haven't showered in three days, and my baby developed a milk allergy so she is throwing up about once an hour." (Insert nice pat on the hand by the well-meaning older mom, who is looking at you like you have the best job on the planet and she would trade her clean Ann Taylor outfit in a heartbeat to once again smell like vomit all day, while you're thinking, "Over before you know it? It better be.")

Young moms live in a perpetual state of "what's next?" We are constantly looking ahead to the next stage of our kids' devel-

opment: nursing→rolling over→teething→sitting up→baby
food→crawling→finger food→pulling up→walking→ talking (sort of)→getting rid of the pacifier (this happens early
in the flow chart for firstborns, much later for subsequent
children)→two naps to one nap→really talking (your ear
off)→potty training→preschool→alphabet→prodigy
development. . . .

And because every stage has its struggles, a little thought
embeds itself in our gray matter: "If I can just make it to
_____, this will get so much easier." We mentally live in
tomorrow while simply managing today. We forget to relish
the charms of the present, allowing them to be overshadowed
by our daily challenges.

Listen: an impossibility has occurred in my house. My
baby son Gavin, who acted like a jaguar his entire first day
of Mother's Day Out at age three, started middle school this
month. (As I typed that, tears burned for the twentieth time
over this madness.) I simply cannot believe it. Middle school.
The subject of every third *Dateline* episode.

I am realizing that my kids are going to actually grow
up. I was lying with Gavin in his top bunk the other night,
and he raised his arm and said, "Mom? Smell this. My pits
are starting to reek." This is happening. My boy who used
to smell like baby powder now stinks like the inside of a
trash can.

As usual, Jesus had something brilliant to say about living in the present: "Give us today our daily bread" (Matt.
6:11).

The concept of daily bread has been baiting me for a while.
When God literally gave the Hebrews their daily bread—
dropped from the sky—as they wandered the desert for forty
years, his instructions were explicit: "The people are to go
out each day and gather enough *for that day*" (Exod. 16:4,
emphasis added). He was very clear: no one could hoard
the bread and quail for the future. In fact, any leftovers
were spoiled by the next day, the only exception being the

Sabbath, when they could collect for two days and make room for rest.

God seemed to be saying, "Don't obsess about tomorrow. Live in this day, without worrying about what you'll do or need later. What is nourishment today will be spoiled by tomorrow. Enjoy it today, or enjoy it never."

Keeping one eye on our kids' tomorrow means we only have one eye on their today. We're missing so much. Our kids are going to grow up with or without us, and once it's over, it's over. As I think about my middle schooler, it occurs to me that I might live ninety years on this planet; I'll have him for only eighteen. (Tears again.)

Give us today our daily bread.

I won't spoil this day by grieving what has passed or longing for what has not yet come. I will notice how Caleb slipped this morning and called me Mommy. I will pay attention to the way Sydney pursed her lips, concentrating on her latest art project. I will enjoy the thirty minutes Gavin laid across my lap so I could scratch his back while we watched SpongeBob, not declaring it a waste of time or brain cells. I will look my kids in the eye and listen to what they're saying; I'll try to give real responses. I will continue my habit of going into my sleeping children's rooms every night to tuck their hair back and kiss their cheeks.

You will never have this day with your children again. Tomorrow, they'll be a little older than they were today. This day is a gift. Breathe and notice. Smell and touch them; study their faces and little feet and pay attention. Relish the charms of the present.

Enjoy today, mama. It will be over before you know it.

○ What is that next stage you've been looking forward to?

○ What is most endearing about the stage your child is in?

STEP OUT OF THE SPIN CYCLE

Try to be present today. Look, notice, smell, touch, listen, pay attention, take a picture, write it down.

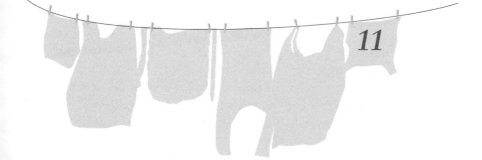

No-Suri

As you would expect from a Christian writer and speaker, I only read the Bible. Except sometimes when I also read *People* magazine and *US Weekly*. (Okay, and so many other books that I have to hide the new ones. It has gotten embarrassing.)

Anyhow, I was reading about Suri Cruise—crazy Tom and mute Katie's baby. The interviewer asked Katie about Suri's temperament, and she said, "Suri is wonderful! She is *always* calm and happy. She seems to have skipped the terrible twos."

Well, how fantastic, Katie. I guess your family lives in a fluffy white cloud in the sky where you slide down rainbows and ride unicorns all day. You must be baffled when you see one of our two-year-olds lie down in the Wal-Mart check-out line and scream until her face turns purple because we wouldn't buy Count Chocula cereal. That must be so confusing to you and Suri. Well someday, Katie, when the other kids call her "Yes-Suri" and "Furry Suri" you needn't worry, because she is "always calm and happy" and clearly immune to the little troubles of life our below-average children lose it over.

For those of us whose kids have refused to skip the terrible twos, I suspect we live in a different world. We live in a microcosm of bipolar mood swings and missed naps and tantrums. And that's just the parents.

Somehow in the middle of this real life we lead—wonderful, challenging, mind-boggling, and exhausting—we got the idea that we had to do it all. Self-sufficient, seemingly autonomous women surrounded us with their seemingly perfect lives, and we assumed the burden of young motherhood was ours alone to carry and carry well.

That is a lie.

The savviest mom is secure enough to reach out for help. And let me tell you something, sweet little lambs: we all need help. This idea of raising children totally independently is a Western concept that sounds R-I-D-I-C-U-L-O-U-S to the rest of the world. Elsewhere, women raise their children in community. They nurse each other's babies, for crying out loud. Mothers, grandmothers, and great-grandmothers live under one roof, sharing responsibilities and distributing the workload. The American obsession with individualism certainly has a downside.

I've always loved the pre-Jesus piece of Mary's story, when she was pregnant. The prophecy was not five seconds out of Gabriel's mouth when Mary packed her bags and traveled south to Elizabeth's house. Not only did Elizabeth—also miraculously pregnant—encourage Mary, saying "Blessed are you among women, and blessed is the child you will bear!" (Luke 1:42), but Mary stayed with her for three months. Elizabeth was in her last trimester, a struggle at her advanced age, while Mary was in her first trimester, scared and young.

They needed each other.

Dear one, there is no rule that says you must succeed at your task alone. That is foolishness. Wisdom makes a phone call when motherhood threatens to overwhelm you, or better yet, *before* it threatens to overwhelm you. There are many ways to skin this cat:

- Trade date night with another couple. My girlfriends Christi and Laura have a Saturday night arrangement; one week Christi takes all the kids and Laura goes out with her hubby, and the next weekend they switch. Free and easy.

- Trade a day off with a girlfriend or a small group of them. Set up a little co-op where you take turns keeping the kids—a small price to pay for a whole day off at no cost.

- Share the cost of a sitter. My girlfriend Trina and I shared a nanny for our youngest boys two days a week. It cut the price in half, and those pals lived like little kings with one doting college-aged babysitter.

- Take people up on their offer to help you. I am so serious. Why don't we do this? Trina offered to take my girlfriend Steph's baby one morning a week to give her a break and fulfill her baby craving. And smart Steph said, "Why yes you can."

- Live by parents or grandparents? This is a no-brainer. My girlfriend Jenny sent her kids to spend the day with her husband's grandmother once a week. They called them "Millie Days," and went for years—intergenerational relationships at their finest.

- Use that man who gave you those babies. For years, Brandon's day off was Friday, and he turned it into Daddy Day and gave me a free pass. If your spouse's work schedule is more conventional, be creative. One evening, a Saturday morning, a Sunday afternoon; engineer some time off whenever you can get it.

- Be humble enough to spontaneously call your friend and say, "I am coming over right this second. We'll lock the kids in the backyard. I need reinforcement." Be vulnerable enough even to say, "Can I drop my kids at your house for two hours and reclaim my sanity?"

It takes a village (thanks, Hillary). It has always taken a village. Our culture tricked us into thinking otherwise, but I'm here to dispel that myth. Ask for help—*this is not a sign of weakness*—receive it when it comes, be proactive, and exhale. There is no such thing as Superwoman, only Super-friends and Super-families. None of us are perfect, and we need each other desperately.

Except for Suri, of course.

○ Have you been tricked into thinking you don't need help? If so, how is that working out?

STEP OUT OF THE SPIN CYCLE

Do you see an idea above that might work in your life? What do you need to do to make it happen? Do it.

Seven Times in a Day

(Of Course I'm Not Talking about Sex)

Those who have only birthed one baby, listen up: Here's what will happen with subsequent children. If you go for two, there is a good chance your second will be as compliant as the first. But hear me on this: If you have three, your last one will be a firecracker. Trust me. Ask everyone you know. For some reason, number three is, um, a "handful." I don't know why this is, but it's true. I can take one look at a kid and immediately conclude: "He's the youngest."

This is our Caleb, for sure. In a weird twist, it is also what makes him so endearing. (It reminds me of the day when I brought home straight As for the ten thousandth time, and I watched my mom and younger sister *jump up and down* because she got a D in algebra instead of an F. No, I'm not kidding.)

Anyhow, Caleb has been consistent trouble in church. I suppose "pastor's kid" and "acting out in church" are redundant, but here we are nonetheless. To reset and regroup, he sat with me in the main service a bit. (His comment during Brandon's sermon: "This is way more boring than my church.") But after his re-entry to kid's church, I picked him up and the look on the teacher's face said everything: bad news. After much discipline, we were praying that night in his bed, and Caleb said:

"Dear God, I am really sorry for acting so bad in church this week."

Pause. Pause. (I'm waiting.)

"Okay, and all the other ones."

Your kids might act like shining angels dropped them straight into your arms from the bosom of heaven, and if so, the rest of us don't really like you. But if you have a challenging child, or a stubborn child, or one who refuses to learn his lesson—okay, basically all kids—forgiveness is a peculiar discipline to practice as mothers. When she was born, you thought, "This is the love of my life. I shall cherish her every second of every day, no exceptions and no take-backs." However, living a real life with our kids forces us into this unexpected arena where we must choose to forgive them.

When I was selecting a passage for this topic, I was overwhelmed by how often Jesus commanded this of us:

- "Forgive us our debts, as we also have forgiven our debtors" (Matt. 6:12).
- "Forgive your brother from your heart" (Matt. 18:35).
- "If you hold anything against anyone, forgive him" (Mark 11:25).
- "Forgive, and you will be forgiven" (Luke 6:37).
- "If he sins against you seven times in a day, and seven times comes back to you and says, 'I repent,' forgive

him" (Luke 17:4). *Surely* this one was said to the moms in the crowd.

Don't forget how often Jesus himself forgave individuals, groups, nations, and the entire world throughout the Gospels. I don't know where Jesus got the reputation of being impossible to please, but no one has ever been slower to judge and quicker to forgive.

Anger, disappointment, hurt feelings, rip-your-hair-out frustration . . . these are part of the motherhood buffet. There are times we will look at our children and—I'm just going to say it—not even like them. This is usually following a nasty confrontation, or after your darling says, "I hate you!"

Human nature handles anger in such destructive ways. We lash out, scream, withhold love, or punish with silence, particularly if that's how our parents treated us. But according to Jesus, it is our high responsibility as Christ-followers to forgive, and this isn't just an adult arena; it is a necessary requirement of motherhood for us to forgive our children.

When our kids fail, discipline is in order, of course. (Not the snapping-twig-screaming-mental-patient kind of discipline, but that's another devotional.) However, when they apologize, when they show remorse or receive our instruction, the most important thing we can say is: "I forgive you."

In my immature moments when my son's failures have worn down my mercy, the situation worsens when I withhold forgiveness. I know because he'll loiter, watching for a sign that we're okay, that I still love him, and when he can't handle my silence any longer, he'll ask, "Mom? Are you still mad at me?"

We discipline in order to teach our kids responsibility, self-control, godliness, obedience—all important. But we forgive in order to teach them mercy, compassion, unconditional love, kindness—all equally important.

While I was still a sinner, Christ died for me. Not after I'd shown potential for improvement, not once I cleaned up my act, not when I earned his forgiveness. He loved me in my own spiritual infancy, full of failure and disobedience. He forgave me for the same mistakes I made over and over and over. He showed me mercy for every misstep and stuck by me when I refused to learn my lesson. When I pitched fits, acted out, and ruined perfectly good opportunities for obedience, Jesus forgave.

We must look at our children and see their value before their failures, their redemption instead of their mistakes. We discipline and forgive, discipline and forgive. Our body language, our words, everything must communicate: *You are exonerated.* We show them that failure is not a deal-breaker and love is supreme. In that, we demonstrate the mercy shown us by Christ when he told us: "Friend, your sins are forgiven" (Luke 5:20).

○ Do you have a child who tests the limits of your forgiveness?

○ You cannot control his behavior, only yours. How have your last few confrontations ended? What did your words and body language communicate?

STEP OUT OF THE SPIN CYCLE

Talk to your child today and confess your mistakes (such as anger, yelling, or punishing silence). Set a new tone and give your child a clean slate.

Jesus the Magic Genie

Three seconds after our oldest son decided to play soccer, our youngest son declared his devotion to the sport. Understand we adhere to the holy trifecta of sports: football, basketball, and baseball, in that order. Soccer is fine if you're Brazilian or a double-arm amputee who needs a sport, but besides that, why would you pick it over football??

But this is not about us. It's about Caleb, who took one look at Gavin's cool uniform, shin guards, tall socks, sweet headband, and new cleats and fell hopelessly in love with soccer. Or I should say soccer paraphernalia. He talked us into signing him up and proceeded to wear the entire getup for five straight days. And to bed. The shin guards were also worn as forearm shields, the headband turned into a "thigh band" (don't ask), and evidently the cleats doubled as dress shoes. The whole uniform was his singular source of entertainment for weeks.

What wasn't as entertaining to Caleb was the actual game of soccer. That shine wore off nearly immediately. After one practice, he informed us we need not bother taking him to those anymore, because he already knew how to play. He wanted to quit every game at halftime. Once, when he was supposed to be playing, we found him on the other team's side eating their snacks. He wasted valuable game time practicing his break-dancing moves instead of that bothersome running up and down the field.

The sweet soccer gear? Check.

The sport itself? Not so much. (Good-bye, $150.)

The day after Jesus's miraculous feeding of the masses with five loaves and two fish:

> They got into the boats and went to Capernaum in search of Jesus.
>
> When they found him on the other side of the lake, they asked him, "Rabbi, when did you get here?"
>
> Jesus answered, "I tell you the truth, you are looking for me, not because you saw miraculous signs but because you ate the loaves and had your fill. Do not work for food that spoils, but for food that endures to eternal life, which the Son of Man will give you. On him God the Father has placed his seal of approval."
>
> John 6:24–27

Jesus's public ministry was something of a sensation to the Jews. Matthew tells us five thousand men were there, not including women or children, so you can imagine the mob scene this was. These people were commoners, mostly poor, and Jesus was making a serious splash. By the thousands, they were following him, looking for him, asking him a bazillion questions.

But why?

Verse 15 tells us they wanted to make Jesus their fancy new king.

Verse 26 shows us they wanted more things from him, like free food.

Verse 30 says they wanted to see more neat tricks.

So Jesus sliced open their motive and laid it bare: "You're looking for me because you want something from me." It was the earliest demonstration of the prosperity gospel: "Follow Jesus, Get Cool Stuff." They wanted the snazzy Jesus paraphernalia without playing the Jesus game.

Cue the physical-to-spiritual transition that Jesus always nailed: "Don't work for food that perishes, but for food that is everlasting. Don't love me for what you can get, but love me for who I am: the keeper of eternity, sealed with the imprint of God himself. You're impressed with bread, but you have no idea what I can really give you."

My stars! This applies to American Christians maybe even more than it applied to those Jews. They, at least, had the excuse of ignorance: Jesus had only been on the scene for five seconds. We have the entire gospel, prophesied and fulfilled, with two thousand years of teachings layered on top, and we are still coming to Jesus for free bread, for promotions, for sold houses, for the utterly temporary.

We ask insincere questions like the Jews ("Hey, when did you get here?"), but Jesus wasn't born yesterday. He knows what we really want from him. It's evident by how we live, what we hang on to, what we refuse to release, where we spend our money, what we value, what we abandon him over, what our dreams are.

> Then they asked him, "What must we do to do the works God requires?" Jesus answered, "The work of God is this: to believe in the one he has sent."
>
> John 6:28–29

At first blush, this sounds simple. Whew! Just believe? Super! I believe! Yessiree. I'm a believer, believe you me. Sure we believe, of course we do. Except this is actually the highest bar of discipleship in the history of leaders and their followers. Because if we really believe Jesus is God's Son, then we must believe in his new world order. You can't have the first without the second.

Which means we couldn't possibly turn a blind eye to the poor or declare "comfort and safety" our top priority. If we really believed, then we'd never be happy living healthy, affluent lives while ignoring the 25,000 people who will die of starvation that same day. Once we are believers, we can't begrudge our enemies or live a totally self-absorbed life. Believing in Jesus means transformation—how could it mean anything less? One who says, "I believe" and lives for herself doesn't believe at all.

Jesus was right: Believing in him is truly the work of God. It's the work of justice and compassion and mercy. It's the work of sacrifice and love and sharing. It's the hard work of representing Jesus on this planet so that a watching world catches a glimpse of God's character. It's about Jesus the redeemer, not Jesus the magic genie. Belief is confirmed by what we think about and proved by what we do. It's the simplest and hardest truth of the kingdom.

This has *everything* to do with parenting, because the kind of disciple I am dictates the kind of mother I am. I am a mom who is passionate about the work of God, or I'm not. My kids will surely know the difference. I'll teach my children to elevate themselves or I'll teach them to love the kingdom; those are mutually exclusive. If I truly believe, then my kids belong to Christ and my highest calling is to see them into his good care. My work is to present them to Jesus as single-minded disciples, prepared and equipped to live out their mission.

If I believe, I create a house of grace.

If I believe, my children will see me forgive and ask forgiveness.

If I believe, my kids will care about this troubled planet Jesus was willing to die for.

May we all be true believers.

○ What did you pray for today? What does it tell you about why you turn to Jesus? Is it more for what you need, or because you love him?

STEP OUT OF THE SPIN CYCLE

Go look at what's on your calendar this week. This month? If belief in Jesus and how we live are totally linked, how would you assess your belief? How you spend your time and money is a great indicator.

The Cannibalization of Me

Okay, truth-telling time. My friends laughed at me as I wrote this book, because it made me terribly sappy. I've been desperately grabby with my kids, and I've lost all semblance of being *with it*. (Gavin: "Mom? Could you please stop waving at the bus?" That's right. I'm *that* mom, standing on the porch in my pajamas, waving at the middle school bus.) I have no idea when I forgot the rules on how to behave. I think it was about the time I signed my contract on this book.

However, I'm looking backward through slightly rose-colored glasses. The fatigue has receded, and I tend to remember early childhood in fuzzy, warm ways. The truth is, that stage of parenting was a little traumatic for me. Because no one told me not to, I had a baby every two years, and it was truly the Mother Load. I remember feeling panicky and desperate, overwhelmed and lost. I forgot what I used to love. My husband would ask me a basic question like, "Where do you want to go for dinner?" and I would blank; not that I couldn't think of a restaurant, but I couldn't recall a preference. I felt uninteresting and uninspiring; my inner diva had gone missing. When I try to remember my deep thought life during that season, there is only a black hole of diapers, schedules, and Elmo.

There was a "me" buried somewhere under "mom," but I struggled to find her. The role of young mother is so encompassing it threatens to eclipse every other title: wife, friend, daughter, professional, *woman*. Some of that is just how it is. It's the most demanding season of parenting, and no amount of fussing is going to change that. We can't have it all, and assuming our other roles should receive the same percentage of our energy as young motherhood is unrealistic.

However, no one role can take all of you without some sacrifice of the others. When we make our children the center of our universe, we do so at the expense of our other relationships. We will fall out of touch with our husbands, our friends, and ourselves when kids consume everything.

Jesus made a rather shocking statement about relational priorities as he sent the disciples out to minister, with the first century version of "cutting the apron strings":

> Anyone who loves his father or mother more than me is not worthy of me; anyone who loves his son or daughter more than me is not worthy of me.
>
> Matthew 10:37

Sheesh. Anyone whose idea of Jesus involves him loving the kittens and petting the lambs has obviously never read the Gospels.

There is a central truth Jesus is getting at that should resonate with us, moms: There is a you that exists only in Jesus, and that identity is beyond the margins of our other roles. The central makeup of you—your gifts, passions, talents, personality, purpose—these were woven into your DNA before time began. Before you were a daughter, a sister, a wife, or a mother, you belonged to God. You were his idea. You'll still be his daughter after your parents and kids are gone. You have a purpose outside of your husband's. When you stand before Jesus one day, it won't be as someone's mom or wife, or as your parents' daughter. It will just be as *you*.

Jesus is warning us not to allow our other relationships to cannibalize our identity. He didn't say, "Don't love your parents and kids"; he said, "Don't love them more than me." Let me tell you something: If we kept this straight, if Jesus received our primary allegiance, we'd never lose ourselves again. How could we?

We'd be in constant touch with our belovedness and redemption.

Jesus would never let us forget our gifts and passions; he put them there.

We'd have a grip on perspective and be less likely to get consumed or distracted.

We would remain attached to the source of strength and peace.

If we loved Jesus more than anyone else, we would be the best possible mothers, the wives of our husbands' dreams. We'd maintain our sparkle, our flair, our laughter. We'd remember our favorite restaurants and get over ourselves. We would remain anchored in the tempest of early childhood, neither losing our way nor losing our minds.

The "you" buried under "mom" is vital, essential, important. Hang on to her. Make sure she gets plenty of face time with Jesus. He'll remind her who she is.

○ Are you lost? Which relationship has suffered most from your absence?

STEP OUT OF THE SPIN CYCLE

However you answered, that relationship needs more of you (even if the answer is "myself"). How can you reallocate your time this week? What specifically will you do?

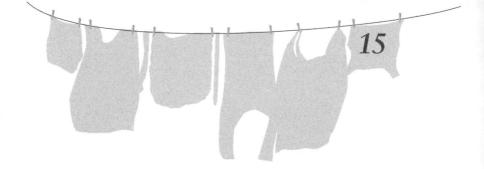

First Century Camping

I have a better job than I had the insight to dream of. I spent my parents' money on a worthless college degree, *because who knows what she wants to do when she's eighteen years old?* Anyhow, God mercifully intervened and now I write books and Bible studies, and travel and speak for a living. I study the Bible and teach and tell funny stories and get paid for it. It's almost too good to be true.

Except for the "traveling" part of travel.

The teaching and human interaction? Love it. The airports and delayed flights and suitcases and quart-sized bags for liquids and middle seats and layovers and missed soccer games and time away from family and a cancelled flight that landed me on a four-hour BUS RIDE from Charlotte to Atlanta instead of the thirty-five-minute connecting flight I paid for, causing me to miss my first two sessions of the conference? Don't love. So my favorite sight is flying into Austin, when the UT Tower and Royal Stadium and Frost Bank and Town Lake come into view. I always have the same glorious thought: *almost home.*

> Now on the last day, the great day of the feast, Jesus stood and cried out.
>
> John 7:37 NASB

Okay, wait.

The feast referred to was called the Feast of Booths (or Feast of Tabernacles). It was the final festival out of the six God had established through Moses. The Feast of Booths was seven days when the Jews lived in booths—like huts—made of tree branches and leaves, "so that your generations may know that I had the sons of Israel live in booths when I brought them out from the land of Egypt" (Lev. 23:43 NASB). For that week, they experienced the desolate state out of which God advanced their ancestors, who lived under similar canopies for forty years in the desert after God liberated them from Egypt through Moses.

The people developed special traditions to mark the end of this festival. The most spectacular was the water-drawing ceremony. Imagine a whole parade of worshipers and flutists led by the priest to the pool of Siloam. The priest has two golden pitchers. One is for wine. He fills the other with water from the pool. As the flutes play, a choir of Israelites chants Psalm 118. The whole procession heads back to the Temple through the Water Gate. A trumpet sounds as the priest enters the Temple area. He approaches the altar where two silver basins are waiting. He pours wine into one, as a drink offering to the Lord, and water from the pool of Siloam into the other. The whole ceremony, with the parade and flutes and singing, was such a joyful occasion that one of the ancient rabbis wrote: "Anyone who has not seen this water ceremony has never seen rejoicing in his life."[1]

---

1. http://jewsforjesus.org/publications/newsletter/1998_10/tabernacles.

This happened on the eighth day, called "the great day" of this festival, because the Jews returned to their homes from their temporary huts, much like their ancestors entered the Promised Land at the end of their exile. After seven days in booths, coming home inspired much gratitude for God's deliverance and provision, and together they celebrated the water ceremony in remembrance.

So now you can see the wisdom in Jesus's next words as he proclaimed this publicly in the Temple on "the great day":

> If anyone is thirsty, let him come to Me and drink. He who believes in Me, as the Scripture said, "From his innermost being will flow rivers of living water."
>
> John 7:37–38 NASB

It was as shocking as it was thrilling. He was transforming the meaning of their holy days, their sacred elements. It would be like shouting at the lighting of the Christmas tree in Rockefeller Plaza in NYC: "Hey! I am the true tree! Hang your lights on me and they will never burn out!" How brilliant that Jesus chose the last day of the Feast of Booths to proclaim this truth. It was the day people celebrated provision, security, kept promises, and God's deliverance.

It was the day they came home.

Jesus was communicating: "As happy as this day feels, as joyous the celebration, as meaningful the ceremonies, you'll never be thirsty again with me. This is just water poured into a basin, but through me, living waters will flow from your innermost being. You may be coming home today from your booths, but I'll take you home with me for eternity."

I love this discourse, because it rings so familiar. There is something so accurate about streams of living water flowing through us because of Jesus. My husband once explained a relationship with Christ by saying, "It's like coming home." Jesus picked a happy day, a day of celebration, to compare himself to. It was a perfect teaching moment.

I think of you, young mom, working so hard to create a happy home, a place where your family exhales when they walk in the door. You might have come from a desert; maybe you practically lived in a booth growing up. Perhaps you spent years of your life lost, exiled, unstable, or wandering. Maybe you never knew a happy home; yours was a wilderness childhood. What you wouldn't have given for a cheery homecoming somewhere, with someone who loved you ridiculously and met all your needs.

"If anyone is thirsty, let him come to me and drink," says Jesus.

Not only is Jesus the stability you've always wanted, but he transforms you into a woman with rivers of living water flowing from your innermost being. He creates the peace in you that you find in him. Your children observe the strength in you they'll later discover in him. No matter how long you have been lost or how lonely your wilderness is, come to Jesus.

It's like going home.

O Have you been dry, lost, or exiled—either while growing up or right now? Describe your experience.

O Have you felt the joy of "coming home"? How were you delivered?

STEP OUT OF THE SPIN CYCLE

Do something special today that will make your children and husband happy to live in your home.

16

A Half-Filled Bag of Doritos

There were so many elements of parenting I was unaware of when I signed up for it. In the earliest stage, my romantic notion of motherhood was hijacked by such delights as breast pumps, sitz baths, and hemorrhoids. Everyone forgot to tell me I'd still look six months pregnant after I delivered, and I'd need to wear adult diapers for three weeks. I found it troublesome that my hair fell out in clumps and my nipples looked like ground beef.

Lately, it has become clear that being a mom means repeating all my years of schooling. I've been in kindergarten and first grade three times in the last six years, and I recently started middle school. I'm on my second round of fourth grade—and my scores are improving, I'm glad to report. (My husband received second place in the science fair last year. We were so proud.) Friends, if you have any inquiries about Chinese immigrants, Paul Revere, Princess Diana's early years, the Alaskan rain forest, geckos, the effect of over-inflation on the bouncing capacity of a soccer ball, or a (biased) summary of Texas history, please call me, because I—um, I mean my kids—have done twenty thousand hours of research on these and other fascinating topics.

There is simply no end to the giving that motherhood requires. Early on, it's as physically demanding as running a daily marathon. In preschool, the emotional energy required caused one of my girlfriends to post on Facebook one day: "GREAT MERCIFUL HEAVENS! I'm engaged in a word war with a three year old. And he's winning. Someone please come save me or his blood is on your hands."

Later, you might have an emotional breakdown right in the middle of your second school project of the week, which has cost you $112 and your entire Saturday (guilty). We give all our time, every possible sacrifice, and each day to the needs of our children, and sometimes it leaves us gasping.

> Give, and it will be given to you. They will pour into your lap a good measure—pressed down, shaken together, and running over. For by your standard of measure it will be measured to you in return.
>
> Luke 6:38 NASB

This is a slice of Jesus's Sermon on the Mount. He discussed loving, sharing, lending, and forgiving others, and summed it up with that statement. "Giving" is the umbrella under which the entire Christian life exists. It is the basis of faith, commissioned by God and perfected by the example of Jesus.

But that teensy-tiny part of me that is selfish (roll eyes here) asks, "How much can I possibly give before I burn out?" After tons of teaching on loving your enemies, sharing with the poor, lending to the questionable, forgiving your offenders—giving, giving, giving—Jesus wisely explained the flip side of the coin. Give, and it will be given back. It is replenishable to the degree it is given in the first place: give abundantly, receive abundantly . . . withhold, and expect the same treatment.

Jesus used an illustration that made perfect sense to the average first century Jew. It was common practice to buy a measure of dry goods, like grain. Stingy, greedy vendors had a habit of pouring grain into the container as loosely as possible so it appeared full, but they actually shorted their customers the full measure. It's the ancient equivalent of opening a giant bag of Doritos and finding it half-empty, the container a total bait and switch of air and plastic.

It is so easy to give like this to our kids and withhold our whole attention, shorting them the full measure of affection. None of us mean to, but the enormity of their need is sometimes paralyzing. There's just so much of it. Certainly there are tasks outside of parenting that require our attention, but when motherhood is the hat we're wearing, it's too easy to listen with one ear, to shoo them away, to fill their container as loosely as possible so we can just get through the day.

Jesus promised when we choose sacrifice and love—the fullest measure of giving—it will be returned, not like a half-filled bag of Doritos, but "pressed down, shaken together, and running over." This was the habit of the most generous vendors, who poured in the grain, shook it down flat, poured in more, pressed it down to make even more room, then poured it so full it spilled over the top. Jesus said this is how "they will pour it into your lap."

My "they" are three needy children, who require more from me than I could've ever imagined. But that same "they" have already begun to give back.

Pressed down: Gavin to us last week, "During Dad's sermon, I felt God speaking to me. I can't explain it, but I want to sell a bunch of my gaming stuff and give the money to someone who needs it."

Shaken together: Sydney in the car, "Sheesh! How am I going to choose my career? Run an orphanage? Build a homeless shelter that has REAL beds for a change? Be a doctor for people who can't afford one? There are just so many people to help, Mama."

Running over: As I prayed with Caleb last night, he crawled into my lap and wrapped his arms around my neck and said, "Mom? When we pray together, let's always hug."

Let's fill our children's containers to the brim—pushing through exhaustion, beyond fatigue, and past boundaries—and ours will surely run over too.

○ What time of day or what distraction (computer, TV, cleaning) tempts you to fill your kids' containers only half-full?

STEP OUT OF THE SPIN CYCLE

Today, choose to forgo the distractions or push through the daily slump when your kids usually get only half of you. Let this be a full measure day.

Tequila Sunrise

A few years ago, my friend Jennifer taught Vacation Bible School in a low-income part of Nashville. Each night, the kids memorized a verse and received a prize for correctly reciting it the next day.

One particular girl named—I couldn't possibly make this up—*Tequila Sunrise* came fired up to share her memorized verse, which (accurately) was, "He is not here. He is risen, just as he said!" As she hopped up and down and prepared to earn her prize, she shouted out:

"He ain't here! He's in prison, just like he said!"

After I picked myself up off the floor, I thought about Tequila (wishing she belonged to me so I could enjoy her every day for the rest of my life) and her understanding of who Jesus was. Jesus in prison made perfect sense to her, because it fit her context. She filtered God's Word through her own life experiences and placed the Messiah in the clink.

Jesus faced a similar struggle with his new followers. The Jews had a distorted context for leadership. They were ruled by:

- powerful Romans who occupied their Holy Land by force and ruled with fear.
- turncoat Jews who bartered their loyalty to the Romans for power and regional influence.
- self-righteous, legalistic Pharisees and Sadducees who enforced impossible spiritual laws with legions of judgment.

These were the only types of leaders they'd ever known—oppressive, greedy, traitorous, and falsely pious. They had no precedent for Jesus. Knowing this, Jesus created a dazzling teaching moment. He took the disciples on a walk. From Bethsaida, they traveled 25 miles north to Caesarea Philippi, which was quite pagan. A general of Alexander the Great originally settled it in 323 BC and established a decidedly Greek culture.

Back then, a cave was discovered where the snowmelt from nearby Mount Hermon flowed underground and surfaced at the base of a high cliff. This cave was declared sacred and dedicated to Pan, the Greek god of herds, shepherds, and nature. A cult center called Paneas was built on this site.

In 20 BC, Paneas was added to the kingdom of Herod the Great, the pro-Roman king of Judea. He built a temple dedicated to Augustus Caesar next to Pan's temple. When Herod died, Paneas became part of his son Philip's territory. Philip named the city "Caesarea Philippi" and declared it the capital of his kingdom.[2]

This was an unlikely destination for a wandering Jewish rabbi and his disciples. I imagine the disciples staring at those two pagan shrines—one to Pan, one to Caesar—built into the

2. http://www.ourfatherlutheran.net/biblehomelands/galilee/banias.htm "Caesarea Philippi" (August 2005).

side of the rock cliff, the carved niches containing all kinds of idols. Jesus had an important lesson to teach them. He needed the right backdrop, and this was it.

> When Jesus came to the region of Caesarea Philippi, he asked his disciples, "Who do people say the Son of Man is?" They replied, "Some say John the Baptist; others say Elijah; and still others, Jeremiah or one of the prophets."
>
> Matthew 16:13–14

People have always identified Jesus with their personal heroes, legends, and stories—as well as with their own parents, pastors, and leaders. Harsh, compassionate, impossible to please, legalistic, kind, unfaithful, trustworthy, wrathful . . . we assign Jesus the labels we've known. You and I have already done this. As adults, we are finding our conclusions to be right or wrong, enjoying God's true character or unlearning what we have misjudged.

But our children are in this process right now. They are learning who Christ is. They're assigning Jesus an identity through the spirit of their homes and the language of their parents. Who would our children say Jesus is?

> "But what about you?" he asked. "Who do you say I am?"
>
> Simon Peter answered, "You are the Christ, the Son of the living God."
>
> Jesus replied, "Blessed are you, Simon son of Jonah, for this was not revealed to you by man, but by my Father in heaven. And I tell you that you are Peter, and *on this rock* I will build my church, and the gates of Hades will not overcome it."
>
> vv. 15–18, emphasis added

Do you see what Jesus did? He took them to a rock cliff in a godless city ruled by foreign leaders saturated with idol worship, and he reframed their concepts of power, spiritual leadership, and sovereignty. As they stood by that rock representing all the wrong ways, he explained the true rock: the name of Jesus—supernatural, immovable, eternal. What a teacher!

This is our task as mothers. We must think critically about the Jesus our kids are formulating, weed out the inferior concepts, and teach them his true character. If Jesus used an object lesson for adults, we can follow suit for our children.

"Jesus is like this umbrella . . ."

"Jesus is like this tree . . ."

"Jesus is like that mountain . . ."

My girlfriend Christi asked her dad if her salvation was secure when she was about twelve. He walked her to their barn, about half a mile away on their 88 acres. He brought out a stake and mallet and pounded it solidly into the Mississippi soil.

"Try to pull that up, Christi."

When she couldn't even budge it, her dad told her that was like salvation. It was nailed down permanently, unmovable. It was not affected by bad choices or mistakes; Jesus was a permanent presence in her heart, and nothing she could do or stop doing would ever change that. What a teacher!

It was so profound she is still talking about it twenty years later.

We must teach our children who Jesus is any way we can. Assuming they will pick it up from church is irresponsible; there is no other relationship more important for us to nurture. What good is it if our kids graduate summa cum laude but still think Jesus is angry, irrelevant, judgmental, or unreal? They must know how he held babies and raised children from the dead. They have to hear how he was the life of the party and loved the outcasts. They need to understand he wasn't killed or caught but that he laid his life down willingly, when he was ready. When Jesus asks our children, "Who do you say I am?" . . .

It's our job to make sure they have an answer.

STEP OUT OF THE SPIN CYCLE

Think of a concrete way to teach the character of Jesus to your children today. Find a way to demonstrate his love, his presence, his joy, or his protection.

18

My Empty Nest Syndrome

I recently had a full-blown, tears-down-the-face cry in the car about my son going to college. I can't fathom his empty room; I can't bear the thought of my youngest son navigating without him. Gavin makes us laugh forty times a day, and pretending to act normal with 20 percent of our family gone is ludicrous. All I can think about is Gavin as a toddler, Gavin as a kindergartener, Gavin singing a solo in the fourth grade musical. I can't stand the idea of giving him up. He's not ready for college. Will he call me enough? Will he tell us what is really going on? What if he needs us and we're too far away?

These miseries were still ping-ponging around in my head when I walked in the door with tearstains etched on my face.

Brandon: What's wrong?
Me: I'm so depressed.

Brandon: Why? What happened?
    Me: Gavin is going to college and I am going to
        miss him so much I can't take it.
Brandon: (long pause) He's eleven.
    Me: But he's going someday!
        (Waaaaaaaaaaaaaaaaaaaaa!)
[Brandon flees to neighbor's house where people aren't spilling actual tears over something that won't happen until 2016. Bless him.]

There is something so precious, so wonderful about the "raising children" years. I live with a constant awareness that *this is it*. We have this short season with them, and it's flying by. But although these years are few, they are critical. The years our kids spend in our homes literally determine who they'll become. Our kids are moldable and impressionable; they are forming worldviews and building habits. In fact, the human brain is not fully developed until late adolescence, and in the case of males sometimes not until early adulthood (duh).[3]

This is actually wonderful news for moms. Our children will never be as teachable as they are right now. In the future, habits will be much harder to break and ideas will be entrenched. They'll be more rigid in their perspectives and new concepts will not incorporate as easily. Spiritual sensitivity is at an all-time high in children; 85 percent of all believers choose Jesus before the age of fourteen. After that window, only 15 percent are flexible enough in their belief system to make room for Christ (of those over age thirty, the number drops to only 4 percent).

Right now, our kids are like clay in our hands. We are their number one influence until adolescence. They are teachable, adaptable, and flexible. Their first reaction isn't suspicion or skepticism, and faith will never come more easily. Apparently, this has always been true:

At that time the disciples came to Jesus and asked, "Who is the greatest in the kingdom of heaven?"

---

3. http://www.childdevelopmentinfo.com/development/piaget.shtml.

He called a little child and had him stand among them. And he said: "I tell you the truth, unless you change and become like little children, you will never enter the kingdom of heaven. Therefore, whoever humbles himself like this child is the greatest in the kingdom of heaven."

Matthew 18:1–4

Listen, just because Jesus wasn't a dad doesn't mean he didn't fully understand children. Don't you love his answer? Obviously, the disciples were trying to position themselves as Top Follower, securing their place of honor in the kingdom. It was so like Jesus to pull a child into the circle and say, "Here. Be like this kid or you'll never be great in my world."

Humble, simple, moldable, dependent—children are so much closer to the kingdom than you and me. And while that casts a dubious shadow over our capacity for transformation (our flexibility can be summed up in two prefixes: *un-* and *re-*, as in unlearning, undoing, recovering, rethinking), it is excellent news for the babies we're raising. They have no need for *un-* and *re-* yet. They are blank pages, unscripted and receptive. Two reasons to celebrate this:

1. We haven't messed them up yet! (There's still time, of course, but hoorah for now.)
2. Discipling our kids and introducing them to Jesus will never be easier.

They're hanging on your every word, mama. They accept what you tell them. They are humble enough to believe in a Savior who walked on water and knew them before they were born. They have much space for the concept of redemption. They are able to incorporate a worldview that begins and ends with a heavenly Father. They trust you without the urge to deconstruct everything you believe. They are low-hanging fruit for the kingdom.

The silver lining about their future non-flexibility is this: Having received Jesus and adopted his love for this planet early on, our kids will be less likely to abandon him later. Their spiritual DNA is solidifying right now. They'll not easily alter the beliefs and convictions integrated during their formative years. A child who falls in love with Jesus the One and Only—his character, not just his rules—is likely to stay the course the rest of his or her life.

> Train a child in the way he should go, and when he is old he will not turn from it.
>
> Proverbs 22:6

○ What spiritual questions have your kids already asked you?

STEP OUT OF THE SPIN CYCLE

Bring up a spiritual conversation with your children today. Start with something tangible they understand, like nature, families, or friends.

The Santa Debacle

We're not parents who staged an elaborate Santa charade. We left the obligatory cookies and milk, and of course, used the standard Santa Threatening Technique from October on ("If you don't knock that off, Santa will skip our house and Christmas will be ruined. Pass the butter."). Santa always brought each kid one present, because, by golly, I refused to let him get all the credit for *my* hours of shopping, wrapping, and general holiday madness. When Santa foots the Christmas bill, Santa can get the Christmas glory.

However, even in our moderate Santa home, there came the inevitable season when our kids doubted the whole concept. Of course, there is always that one bratty kid who blurts out, "Santa isn't real! It's your parents!" in every elementary classroom, but even without that future felon, intuitive children eventually doubt that a fat man in a ridiculous costume pulled by flying caribou visits every house in the world in one night.

We decided to tell our kids the truth when they asked, so when Sydney popped the question, I tried the diversion technique that staved off Gavin for another year. ("Do *you* think he's real?") Gavin bit until the next Christmas, but Sydney wasn't having it.

"That's not what I asked, Mama."

"Remember about the Christmas magic and the thing with the time warp?"

"Mom."

"Okay, it's me and Daddy."

"I knew it." Sigh. Silence. Pondering. Thinking what liars we are. "You know, Mama? I really wanted to believe, but I just couldn't buy those floating reindeer." If Santa could lose the reindeer, I think his attrition rate for believers would immediately improve. They're dragging his legend into the gutter.

Doubt. A natural companion to Santa. And to God. With anything unseen, there comes a moment when even the staunchest believer says, "Really?" Not only is doubt common, but Jesus made some room for it.

Back story: John the Baptist was more than Jesus's cousin; he was the forerunner whose entire purpose was announcing Jesus's coming. His conception was nearly as miraculous as Jesus's, and angels and prophecy surrounded his debut too.

He was selected for one objective: get everyone ready for Jesus's public ministry. John spent his whole life in the desert, waiting, and when he stepped forward, his ministry of preparation was so powerful, people constantly wondered if he was the promised Messiah. No sooner did he baptize Jesus, thereby inaugurating his mission, than John was thrown into prison by Herod, locked away from observing Jesus's public unveiling.

So for a guy whose *entire function* was to announce Jesus, this was surprising:

When John heard in prison what Christ was doing, he sent his disciples to ask him, "Are you the one who was to come, or should we expect someone else?"

Matthew 11:2–3

John's time was almost up, and he knew it. In his final communication with Jesus, John—facing death and the completion of his earthly task—sent his last question. He was mostly sure, pretty sure, almost sure, but doubt prompted him to make *really* sure.

Does that relieve you like it does me, girls? If JOHN THE BAPTIST had moments of doubt, we can stop freaking out over ours. I'm not endorsing chronic skepticism, but Jesus asks us to "fix our eyes not on what is seen, but on what is unseen" (2 Cor. 4:18), and that's no small request. Maybe that's why God places such high value on faith; it's difficult to trust in an unseen God. Add to that misrepresentation by his people, the unsightly edges of his Church, and the manipulation of his Word, and we'll inevitably struggle with doubt at some point.

So surely this disgusted Jesus, right? I mean, if John doubted him, then what hope was there for anyone? Of all the dudes who should know for sure, John topped the list. His hesitation was certain to start a domino effect, and Jesus obviously should chastise him for this ill-timed question.

Jesus replied, "Go back and report to John what you hear and see: The blind receive sight, the lame walk, those who have leprosy are cured, the deaf hear, the dead are raised, and the good news is preached to the poor. Blessed is the man who does not fall away on account of me."

As John's disciples were leaving, Jesus began to speak to the crowd about John: "What did you go out into the desert to see? A reed swayed by the wind? If not, what did you go out to see? A man dressed in fine clothes? No, those who wear fine clothes are in kings' palaces. Then what did you go out

to see? A prophet? Yes, I tell you, and more than a prophet.
This is the one about whom it is written:
  'I will send my messenger ahead of you,
  who will prepare your way before you.'
  I tell you the truth: Among those born of women there has
not risen anyone greater than John the Baptist!"

Matthew 11:4–11

Does that sound like an irritated Savior? Listen, even the
best of God's saints have need for reassurance sometimes.
Jesus said: "Hey! John is not a reed swayed by the wind—
quite the contrary." He was strong, sturdy, stable—his inquiry
was no indicator of weakness. It was a legitimate question,
and Jesus dignified it with the best possible answer, void of
any disapproval.

John could be certain Jesus was the One: just ask the blind,
lame, diseased, deaf, dead, and poor people he restored.

This goes for us too. Have you struggled with doubt, wondering if Jesus really is the One? Needed some divine reassur-
ances? *It's okay.* You're in good company, and Jesus has no
condemnation for the question. Here is how you'll know:

Has Jesus ever opened your eyes, revealing blind spots and
granting clarity?

Have you witnessed anyone emotionally crippled who
began walking again with Christ?

Have you seen God cure people of their greed? Selfishness?
The disease of pride?

Has Jesus overcome your spiritual deafness, speaking redemption into your life?

Have you seen him resurrect a life? A marriage? A family?
A church?

Do you remember your own poverty before Jesus rescued
you with his radical love?

Jesus may be unseen, but evidences of his greatness are
everywhere. When doubt creeps in and you wonder if your
faith has been well placed, just look around. Where there was

healing, there was a Healer. Where there was redemption, there was a Redeemer. Where you saw restoration, there was a Restorer. When someone was rescued, there was a Savior.

Where love won, hope triumphed, and faith conquered . . . Jesus was the hero.

○ Is there a doctrine or particular theology that gives you trouble?

○ What's the greatest evidence of Jesus you've ever seen or experienced?

STEP OUT OF THE SPIN CYCLE

In an age-appropriate way, tell your kids today about the greatest thing you've ever seen Jesus do.

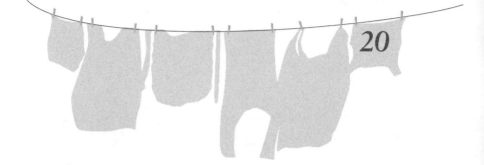

Skorts

It's a Skirt That Acts like Shorts!

I got a phone call from my girlfriend Trina that we have filed in the "hilarious" category. I picked up the phone and knew right away something was wrong:

> Trina: Jen, it's me. I'm in trouble.
> Jen: What's wrong? What happened?!
> Trina: I'm shopping for clothes, and all of a sudden (whispering) I don't know what I'm supposed to wear anymore! I'm looking at an outfit thinking, "That's cute. My sister would wear that," but she's twenty years older than me!
> Jen: Calm down. I'm sure it's not that bad. Is the waistband elastic? Does it have matching embroidery around the sleeves and cuffs?

Trina: HOW DID YOU KNOW?! And it gets worse. . . .

Jen: Please tell me you did not buy suntan pantyhose.

Trina: I'm holding a pair of skorts.

Jen: (gasp) Trina, listen very carefully to me. Put the skorts down and back away slowly. BACK AWAY! Look for the nearest exit!

Trina: But it's a skirt that acts like shorts.

Jen: Stop it!! You're SCARING me! It starts with one pair of skorts, and you think you can handle them. But the next thing you know, you're wearing Easy Spirits and eating dinner at 4:00! That's it. I'm coming right now. Just sit on the floor and wait for me.

I found her in the "Active Woman" department at Penney's, and I barely got her out in time.

Jen: (being gentle yet firm) What happened in there?

Trina: I don't know. I just got so confused. (Wailing) So distracted! There were too many coordinates! I was surrounded! All I could see were embroidered butterflies and cardigans!

Jen: Oh, Trina! You must have been so scared!

Trina: Don't ever let me shop alone again. I get sensory overload and feel the need to dress like my mother.

Jen: Repeat after me: "Clean lines, solids not patterns, basics. BASICS! SIMPLE!" If you want to be a sparkly-pants, it *must* be confined to your accessories. Do you understand?

Trina: This is going into the "hilarious" category, isn't it? You're going to write about this, aren't you?

Jen: (patting Trina gently) Of course I am.

Overload. It gets the best of us. As moms, it's easy to become distracted by worries, guilt, anxiety, busyness, and whatnot. Girls, life is a long journey, so Jesus gave some travel advice: "Stay simple. Travel light." Where we tend to add clutter, Jesus takes the opposite approach.

Jesus said, "Blessed are the pure in heart, for they will see God" (Matt. 5:8).

This word "pure" is from the Greek word *katharos*. It is used 22 times in the New Testament. It carries three separate but cohesive meanings, all under the definition of "clean." I can hear Jesus urging, begging us to *be free*.

Katharos: clean ethically; free from corrupt desire, from sin, and from guilt.

Did you catch that last part? "Clean from guilt." Is it possible to be cleansed from sin but still carry its guilt? Does a baby immediately poop in a clean diaper? Of course it's possible, and it happens all the time. Have you ever asked God to forgive something he has already forgiven? You know you have. That's guilt talking, girls. Since the enemy can't deny us forgiveness from a holy God, he'll try to deny us its freedom. Through guilt, he presses us down with his lies:

"They don't know the real you."

"You'll never change."

"No one else struggles like you."

"You're a failure."

"You may be forgiven, but God is still disappointed."

Enter Jesus, who took our sin with its nasty residual guilt, nailed it on the cross, and conquered it when he rose again. Did you see what his purity, his *katharos* looks like? Not just unstained from sin, but unstained from guilt. Jesus holds us close and says, "You're forgiven. You're clean. You're pure. Completely."

Is there anything more we could ask for? We can spend a lifetime traveling with our guilt dragging behind us, slowing our journey, spoiling our relationships, turning us into defeated mothers—but that's a choice. Jesus allows us to throw our guilt off with abandon by commanding us, "Do not call anything impure that God has made clean" (Acts 10:15).

○ What guilt have you chosen to travel with?

○ What keeps you from leaving it behind? Are you willing to?

STEP OUT OF THE SPIN CYCLE

Cut your guilt loose today. Ask God to liberate you from it, and believe him when he says, "You are free."

Egg Salad Sandwich Disorder
and Road Rage

I have some traits that were stamped into my DNA, pure and simple. For example, my entire family has two volumes: sleeping and loud. Every one of us also has an impressive capacity for melodrama. It's genetic. Also, I was given some OCD tendencies from my dad—not in terms of cleanliness or organization, of course, but when "egg salad sandwich" gets in my head, I *have to have one within the next thirty minutes*, and you can't tell me that isn't some sort of disorder.

I have other qualities I take full blame for. For instance, I have a little problem called "I hate most other drivers." It manifests as road rage. I'm not proud; I'm just owning it. I also have a little bit of a sassy mouth. I mean to be kind and precious all the time, but I get annoyed. And sometimes when I plan on being Mom Extraordinaire, I accidentally vaporize what little patience I have and several people end up crying. These things are mine. They are a teeny cross section of what my husband dubs my "problem areas."

We all have some environmental factors to consider: the ones we were born into. These are the ones that defined us early on. We came to understand them as "the way things are." We were handed these by our culture, our parents, and our experiences. A certain reality was crafted for us, and we adopted a specific identity to manage it. As mothers, this might have created such "givens" as:

- appearance is everything.
- don't talk about emotional issues.
- never admit you're wrong.
- kids should be seen and not heard.

The teachers of the law and the Pharisees brought in a woman caught in adultery. They made her stand before the group and said to Jesus, "Teacher, this woman was caught in the act of adultery. In the Law Moses commanded us to stone such women. Now what do you say?" They were using this question as a trap, in order to have a basis for accusing him.

John 8:3–6

It was tough to be a woman then. I've always wondered where her partner in crime was during this interrogation. Where were *his* accusers? Certainly, Jewish culture laid the burden of guilt at her feet; women were often held accountable for the sins of men. While men could "dismiss" their wives for any reason ("burning dinner" included, true story), women had no divorce rights. Women were not to be acknowledged or spoken to in public—not even a man to his own wife. In fact, women were to walk six paces behind their husbands. (Adorable.)

Standing up tall under these cultural expectations was tough for those ladies. Some of us get that. We grew up in backward environments with double standards. We were taught bigotry, prejudice, hate, oppression, or inferiority. Habits and attitudes develop out of these paradigms, and it's the work of a lifetime to break free from them.

But there is another set of considerations we must plow through in order to settle into the perfect identity Christ offers: the identity we've crafted through our own sin. We have to own this.

> But Jesus bent down and started to write on the ground with his finger. When they kept on questioning him, he straightened up and said to them, "If any one of you is without sin, let him be the first to throw a stone at her." Again he stooped down and wrote on the ground.
>
> At this, those who heard began to go away one at a time, the older ones first, until only Jesus was left, with the woman still standing there.
>
> vv. 6–9

Interestingly, the only person there without sin, innocent enough to actually throw a stone, was Jesus, yet he defended her rather than stone her. With every right available to him, Jesus chose mercy. Hear that, dear ones. Though he has the moral authority to condemn, he doesn't. Jesus's love language is grace; a truth we should all take note of as failed humans.

> Jesus straightened up and asked her, "Woman, where are they? Has no one condemned you?"
>
> "No one, sir," she said.
>
> "Then neither do I condemn you," Jesus declared. "Go now and leave your life of sin."
>
> vv. 10–11

Go and leave your life of sin.

No matter how much your sin has evolved into your very identity, you can be set free. You are not bound by the image you've chosen. You don't have to continue being that person simply because that is how everyone knows you. Jesus doesn't look at us with eyes of judgment. He knew when he came to earth that we were saturated with sin. No surprises there. He's neither shocked nor horrified. He came to set us free.

He came to set *you* free.

He looks much deeper than what others see on your surface. He looks at your history and understands your disappointments. He looks at your future and knows your potential. Most of all, Jesus looks at your heart, free from its protective layers, and he loves you with an intensity you'll never fully understand.

To be stripped of our sinful identities in front of Jesus doesn't bring disgrace. It simply offers him the bare essence of our souls and allows him to clothe us with forgiveness, godliness, and honor. There is no condemnation between Jesus and a woman who faces her sin.

Let's be women, wives, and mothers who are courageous enough to stand bare in front of Christ, owning our failings and confessing our mistakes. Let's be brave enough to admit our junk without laying all the blame at the feet of our fathers, our mothers, our childhood, or our culture. We won't condone bad behavior or the sins against us, but let's acknowledge the reactions, habits, and tendencies that belong to us.

That moment of truth is worth every moment of freedom that comes after it.

○ What is the most unhealthy habit or perspective you were saddled with as a child?

○ What do you need to own today? What is messing up your relationships or robbing you of joy?

STEP OUT OF THE SPIN CYCLE

If there is someone you need to call or apologize to in order to begin this process of freedom, do it. I promise you, you won't regret it.

22

My Missing Inner Saint

The amount of grace marriage requires is unfathomable.

The other day, Brandon and I were discussing the speed dial feature on our cell phones. I remarked that due to the Irrefutable and Universal Law of Speed Dial, voice mail was number one, but naturally, he was number two, followed by a long list of girlfriends. Obviously, the descending order mirrored my relational priorities; he occupies top billing in my heart.

That's when I noticed a cagey look on his face.

"What's your speed dial lineup?" I asked like the innocent dove I am, naïvely assuming that I too was way up in his ranking system, having birthed his children and been an absolute pleasure to live with these fifteen years.

That's when the baloney began. "Oh yes, well, see, I was thinking I'd put you first, so I went ahead and put Tray second" (his number one boyfriend), "then I put in a couple of the fellas. About then I realized I couldn't put you first due to the Irrefutable and Universal Law of Speed Dial, but I was only at number five, and that didn't seem like a worthy number for my beautiful bride. So I put in one more and chose number seven for you. God's number. I'm honoring you."

I stared blankly, trying to channel my inner saint—but she'd gone missing, as she tends to do. "Are you saying I am number seven in your speed dial? And your five boyfriends took precedence over the woman who has sex with you? Do you think for one second I'm buying what you just fed me about putting me first? Do I look like some kind of halfwit? Hey, guess what, kids? Daddy is number one in my heart, and good news! Mommy slid in at number seven on Daddy's roster, just a hair ahead of his insurance agent! Maybe if I birth another namesake I can move up to number six!"

I'm still working on that grace thingy.

Ah, marriage. The kind of union we have affects our children infinitely more than the schools we put them in, the activities we sign them up for, or the church we take them to. Our kids are learning relational habits by osmosis, and statistics say they'll likely imitate what they witness at home.

Grant was a high school student in our youth ministry, and he was the all-American, utterly privileged kid. Talented, smart, athletic, funny; he literally had it all. His parents were superstar volunteers, and the family was central to the life of the church.

When we heard he totally derailed in college and walked away from Christ, we were stunned. Brandon reached out to him:

"Dude, what happened?"

"None of that is real. My perfect parents? The awesome volunteers who were at church four days a week? Yeah, they were the ones who cussed each other out every day and screamed so horribly we had to leave the house. At church, they said, 'Bless you,' but at home they said, 'I hate you.' I'll pass on that fake religion."

When accused of being on the wrong side of good versus evil, Jesus declared:

Every kingdom divided against itself will be ruined, and every city or household divided against itself will not stand.

Matthew 12:25

Outside forces are less of a threat for most families; they readily crumble from the inside out. A civil war leaves more casualties than an outside attack. When God said two become one in marriage, that means we literally injure our own flesh when we tear down our partner. When I stab at my husband's dignity, I might as well sever one of my own limbs. This is why fighting hurts so badly: when I injure my husband, I do it at the peril of my own soul.

And let's not forget the children. We become so blinded by our own selfishness that we fail to see how a contentious marriage affects them. It's easier just to write it off:

"They don't know what's going on."

"They're too little."

"They're not listening."

A house divided against itself will fall, crushing everyone taking refuge under its shelter.

You want to be the mom of your kids' dreams? Want to give them security, health, stability, and happiness? *Love your husband*. Love him so much it's almost embarrassing. Kiss him, hug him, talk about him to your kids like your heart would expire without him. Refuse to let issues fester until you blow like Mount Vesuvius and char everyone. Have sex with him (this alone would solve most of his problems). Tell your children their daddy is a hero and they're the luckiest kids to belong to him. Be his fan. The best gift for your kids is parents who are crazy for each other. (Did I mention have sex with him?)

Love each other well, and your house will stand, sweet friend.

o How is your inner saint behaving toward your husband lately?

STEP OUT OF THE SPIN CYCLE

Use your words to love your husband today. Tell your kids when you tuck them in that their daddy is a hero.

Garbage for Christmas

Christmas '06 was the year I learned that everything made for kids is junk.

Mind you, this was before the Christmas Reform of '08 (four gifts each: something you want, something you need, something to wear, something to read). In 2006 I was still going for it, and by that I mean buying my kids a bunch of garbage they didn't need.

"Garbage" is really the operative word here. Of the obscene amount of gifts we bought, we returned:

- the "planetarium," which projected one red wiggly dot on the wall. Saddest thing ever.
- the telescope that magnified viewed elements by about 2 percent.
- the MP3 player, which played music that sounded slightly worse than a long-distance call from the mountains of Peru on a walkie-talkie.

- segue: the walkie-talkies that emitted a high-pitched squeal for four seconds every time the kids pressed the talk button, causing my husband to throw one fifty yards into the woods.
- the Junior Metal Detector, which had no sensitivity to metal whatsoever, but had a surprising reaction to dog poop every time.

Add at least six other defective toys that were so poorly made I am positive they hired drunken monkeys to man the assembly lines. After the fifth or sixth toy went defunct, Sydney patted my slumped shoulders and said, "It's alright, Mama. It's not your fault everything you bought is lame." My Christmas happiness was salvaged by surprising reactions to second-tier gifts, like socks with toes and a five-dollar flashlight.

I wanted to give my kids incredible presents. I wanted them to realize I took their personalities and hobbies into full account. I hoped they'd feel loved and known, special and thrilled. My desire was to communicate: "I knew just what you wanted and was *so delighted* to give it to you." (What I actually communicated was that I was an ignorant consumer who believed if you paid good money for a product it would work. What a ninny.)

> For everyone who asks receives; he who seeks finds; and to him who knocks, the door will be opened. Which of you, if his son asks for bread, will give him a stone? Or if he asks for a fish, will give him a snake? If you, then, though you are evil, know how to give good gifts to your children, how much more will your Father in heaven give good gifts to those who ask him!
>
> Matthew 7:8–11

Ha! I love Jesus. I read it like this: "If you—though you are stupid—know how to give 'good' gifts to your kids (sarcasm included), how much more will God give *really* good gifts to those who ask him?!"

You know that compulsion we have to make our kids happy? To give them a surprise? To bestow on them something we are positive they'll love? To fulfill a request we've heard them mention over and over? Multiply that by a hundred: that's our God!

The same joy we feel when our kids rip open a present with a thrill, or lose their minds with excitement over some surprise . . . Jesus tells us God experiences that same delight in us. The upside is, while we get sucked into giving second-rate products that quit working the second they are removed from the package, God knows how to give "good gifts" that last, that matter, and that are terribly profound and marvelous.

What a teacher, that Jesus. He appealed to the parent in his listeners. Would you give your baby a rock when he asked for bread? A snake when she asked for a fish? A Commodore 64 when he asked for an Atari? (My husband should go into therapy as often as he's mentioned this.) Of course you wouldn't. Why not?

Because you love to love your children.

The adoration you feel when you watch your sleeping cherubs? God has it for you. Your pleasure at fulfilling one of their little dreams? Jesus shares that feeling for you. Your bursting heart when your kids laugh? God feels the same way about your joy.

There is a reason God referred to himself as our "Father" more than any other title. If we identify with God as a parent, then we might grasp the endlessness of his love, the boundlessness of his affection, the extent of his mercy. We may start to comprehend the depth of his love and the height of his patience. We'll get closer to his heart for us as daughters, jealous for our safety and hungry for our potential.

If you ask for patience, God won't give you exasperation.

If you beg for strength, don't expect to receive more fatigue.

Once you request an extra dose of kindness, God won't hand out irritation.

You are his daughter, beloved and treasured. The extent you love your children is but a whisper of the devotion God has for you.

> Ask and it will be given to you; seek and you will find; knock and the door will be opened to you.
>
> Matthew 7:7

○ When you think about God as a parent, what inaccurate perception of him fades away?

STEP OUT OF THE SPIN CYCLE

What do you need to ask God for today? He is the best gift giver.

SAHM

Sleepy Anxious Hysterical Mama

When Brandon and I started a family, my heart's desire was to stay home. However, since we were making obscene piles of cash, what with my teacher's salary and his youth pastor's check (sarcasm intended), I wasn't able to stay home until my second child, my daughter, was born. Thus I began a new life with an infant and a two-year-old . . . all day.

Seeing how I'd begged for this and cried real tears over it, you'd think I'd be somewhat immune to the "downside" of being an SAHM. But you would be wrong. I was unprepared for the exhaustion, the drain of emotional energy, and the constancy of it all; when Brandon asked about my day once, I snapped, "Oh, me? I set limits and enforced discipline all day long. It was awesome. You?"

In my mind, Brandon was off at his fancy job, eating at restaurants, laughing casually, and kicking his feet up on his desk (he's never done that last one, but it fit my imagined scenario). He did whatever he wanted while I was neck-deep in diapers and tantrums. I slipped into a pit of resentment in record time, keeping tally of the zillion tasks I completed with no acknowledgment.

I told Brandon once: "Do you know I am literally keeping all these children alive? If I was not on this planet, they'd all be unimmunized, starved anarchists with overgrown fingernails who would never have haircuts or gifts for birthday parties!"

I'm sure he couldn't wait to get home every day.

As I was wallowing in self-pity, Brandon popped the imaginary bubble I'd constructed around his perfect life of freedom. He said, "Here's my side of the story. While I'm stuck in pointless meetings with imbeciles, I'm thinking of you watching the kids learn to walk, which I'm missing. While I'm filling out paperwork, getting chewed out by disgruntled parents, and paying invoices, I'm wishing I was you—liberated from the professional grind, spending time with your friends, singing our kids to sleep for naps. My career is not the picnic you've envisioned, but my solace is that I am giving our kids the gift of their mom."

Pffheeeeeeeew (air out of bubble).

[Jesus said,] "So in everything, do to others what you would have them do to you, for this sums up the Law and the Prophets."

Matthew 7:12

I withheld from Brandon the very things I wanted from him: respect, acknowledgment, and gratitude. If I wanted him to notice my efforts at home, I should've started by saying, "Thanks for working so hard today." If I was hoping to receive some credit for bringing three kids to the pediatrician for shots by myself, maybe a better place to start was, "I'm really grateful for all you do for our family."

We can't expect star treatment from our husbands without doling it out liberally ourselves. To do so is horribly unfair.

We aren't competing for the prize of "who works hardest." We work *differently*; both tasks require gargantuan effort, and we each need the labor of the other. We are a team. It's not a contest or a war; we are on the same side.

For a season, Brandon raised the money while I raised the kids. Of course, he parented too, but while he was at the office, I was in mine—a mobile office that included parks, doctors' offices, Little Gym, the backyard, my overstuffed chair in the playroom, the library, Chick-Fil-A, the swimming pool, the kitchen, friends' houses, and the snow cone stand.

Girls, reframe the way you think about your husband's job and the time and energy it requires. He's not slamming back a scotch and water at 11 a.m. in order to make his noon tee-time. He's laboring too, keeping a roof over your babies' heads and supplying the funds for their organic baby food. I know he's never clipped their fingernails once, but you haven't filled out his expense reports, either. Treat him like you'd love to be treated—with appreciation, thankfulness, and compassion.

"This sums up the Law and the Prophets."

○ Do you struggle with a husband who seems free while you're in baby prison? How do you feel?

○ Can you reimagine his workday in realistic terms?

STEP OUT OF THE SPIN CYCLE

A good first step is appreciating your man for what he does. Give it a try when he comes home.

Baby Couture

(Roll Eyes Here)

No one explained the consumer vortex I'd be sucked into once I became a mother. Nor did they warn me that birthing a daughter secured a first-class ticket on the Toddler Trendy Train. I was an innocent lamb; I'd never heard of stores like Lollipops and Gumdrops, Dimples and Dandelions, or Izzy and Ash. The first time I heard the term "baby couture," I snorted Diet Dr Pepper through my nose. Designer baby bedding, silk diaper bags, high-end shoes for kids who can barely walk? Seriously? Listen, if I buy a $400 lamp to match my toddler's custom bedding to "complete her room," you have permission to smack the tarnation out of me.

What on earth? How did we get here? Probably by increments; you start with a Petunia Pickle Bottom bag—totally harmless; your aunt gave it to you. Then before you know it,

BAM! You're buying a $90 outfit for your toddler, who will have a poop blowout the first time she wears it. Huggies will fail you, whether they're under $75 Maddox Jolie-Pitt jeans or $1.50 Garanimal shorts from Wal-Mart.

You know a preschooler doesn't care about name brands and haute couture for the under-five crowd. They're more likely to fixate on their cheap, flammable dress-up clothes they will insist on wearing in public. This is about us, mamas. When we compulsively overspend on clothes that will fit our children for three seconds, we have derailed. Outfitting our children to keep up with the little Joneses starts a vicious cycle they might never be able to break.

Directly after Jesus told the parable of the man who hoarded his stuff, he said to his disciples:

> Therefore I tell you, do not worry about your life, what you will eat; or about your body, what you will wear. Life is more than food, and the body more than clothes.
>
> Luke 12:22–23

An eager, anxious pursuit of the things of this world—even necessary things—is unbecoming to the disciples of Christ. Our craving for the beauty of holiness is inversely proportional to our hunger for the luxuries of this world. That is hard to say and hard to hear, but it's still true. There is a reason Jesus said, "It is easier for a camel to go through the eye of a needle than for a rich man to enter the kingdom of God" (Matt. 19:24).

The more we have, the more we need. The more we accumulate, the more we value it. Jesus said, "Where your treasure is, there your heart will be also" (Matt. 6:21). I used to say, "It doesn't matter what you have. It's what you do with it." But I'm not sure that's true anymore, because we have what we bought, and we bought what we wanted, and that's a heart issue.

Jesus seems to be saying, "Show me the way a person spends her money, and I'll tell you immediately what she really cares about." When we dump irresponsible loads of money on our children—their clothes, bedrooms, toys, activities—what are we teaching them to value? How are we crippling our own priorities?

I'm starting a new writing project/social experiment this fall, and one thing I'm doing is giving away seven things a day out of my home for one month. You know what, girls? It's not even going to be hard. Between our five closets and the toy chests alone, we'll hardly make a dent. That's just gross. When I think about how much money we've spent on nonessential luxuries, I am broken. I'm broken for the misuse of resources when the entire world is starving, naked, and poor. I'm broken to see the evidence of my greed. No one can deny it. Jesus could walk into my home and quickly determine what matters to me.

It's horrifying to confront my own consumerism, and I'm scared of reform.

> Do not be afraid, little flock, for your Father has been pleased to give you the kingdom. Sell your possessions and give to the poor. Provide purses for yourselves that will not wear out, a treasure in heaven that will not be exhausted, where no thief comes near and no moth destroys.
>
> Luke 12:32–33

God is pleased to give us the kingdom: a worldview that holds possessions loosely. The kingdom liberates us from the prison of materialism. It finds its glory in sharing and giving away. It is free from the trap of "keeping up" and is never at risk of losing it all. The kingdom allows us to spend our time, money, and energy on eternal, unfailing treasures that are immune to economic downturns and greed.

That is the kingdom woman I want to be and the kingdom children I want to raise.

Save me, Lord, from myself.

O Are you caught up in the consumer vortex for your kids? What is your motivation for spending like you do?

STEP OUT OF THE SPIN CYCLE

Go through your children's closets and toys and purge. It's time to share with someone.

Mama on a Mission

When my daughter was four, she started having grand mal seizures. For those of you who have had exposure to epilepsy, you know these seizures are utterly terrifying. The horror of watching your child's face contort, her limbs draw up, her body lose all functionality, her breathing become labored . . . it's unspeakable.

After her first seizure, we spent the night in the emergency room. Blood tests, MRIs, a botched spinal tap, EEGs—a night I wish I could forget. After we finally came home, we got Sydney into bed, and her daddy slept on the floor next to her, unwilling to leave her alone. I fell into bed and lost it; with all of my courage and strength expended, my terror for Sydney consumed me. Was it cancer? A tumor pressing against her brain? Why on earth would a perfectly healthy four-year-old with no family history develop seizures?

I desperately cried out to God for her. And kept crying out, until Sydney outgrew the seizures a few years later.

Some of you have a child in crisis—physical, emotional, spiritual, or relational. You are frantic for healing, worried beyond explanation. You've tried everything; you've gone everywhere. There is nothing you won't consider for the wellness of your child.

> Jesus withdrew to the region of Tyre and Sidon. A Canaanite woman from that vicinity came to him, crying out, "Lord, Son of David, have mercy on me! My daughter is suffering terribly from demon-possession."
>
> Matthew 15:21–22

A mom begging Jesus to intercede for her kids is nothing new. Since God created mothers and children, we've been their prime advocates, their staunchest defenders. We'll take down the administration of an entire school district, so help us. We'll make 32 phone calls until the right person calls us back. We'll corner teachers, doctors, and coaches until they hear us out (God help them if they think we're going away). I'd rather be on the wrong side of an AK-47 than a mama on a mission.

> Jesus did not answer a word. So his disciples came to him and urged him, "Send her away, for she keeps crying out after us."
>
> v. 23

Shut that girl up, for crying out loud! This mama was truly on a mission; she hollered at Jesus across the crowds, shameless and aggressive. Jesus's silence was no deterrent. She was hardly going to back down because she had to ask twice.

A good lesson for us, moms: sometimes when we don't get a response in 1.3 seconds, we throw up our hands and declare ourselves "ignored." We give up too soon and we throw in the towel, certain Jesus is being impossible. Persistence is the mark of an advocate; we'll stay the course until we hear from our Savior.

He answered, "I was sent only to the lost sheep of Israel." The woman came and knelt before him. "Lord, help me!" she said. He replied, "It is not right to take the children's bread and toss it to their dogs."

vv. 24–26

Jesus sounds like a real jerk here. Here is this desperate woman begging for her daughter, and he resorts to prejudice and name-calling. How do we make sense of this? Certainly, she was a Canaanite, historically calloused to God. Precious few Canaanites proclaimed him and even fewer obeyed him. To be fair, Jesus pressed on the sincerity of Jews too:

- "Hey, Jesus? Can I go bury my father before I follow you?" "Nope, let the dead bury their own dead."
- "Yo, Jesus. Your mom and brothers are outside waiting to talk to you." "My mother and brothers are those who do the will of my Father." (Ouch.)
- "Jesus? What do I need to do for eternal life?" "Sell everything you own and give it to poor people. Then we'll talk."

He wasn't as warm and fuzzy as you might have been led to believe. There has always been a high cost to discipleship, and Jesus never soft-sold it. With this hysterical mother, I think Jesus was testing her intentions, pushing against her motives. Was she only interested in this foreign rabbi because of his reputation? Was she simply using him? How would she respond once this conversation turned tense or skeptical?

"Yes, Lord," she said, "but even the dogs eat the crumbs that fall from their masters' table" (v. 27). Clever. She took that shot on the chin and conceded her position as an outsider. This gal was persistent. Resisted once, twice . . . three times, four times . . . she kept coming. Jesus, like a hunter, chases faith in his followers so it may become strong and firmly rooted. He is unwilling to impart cheap grace. The buy-in is high, but the payoff is infinite.

Hear that, praying mama? Jesus won't be used and he wasn't born yesterday. He'll burrow down to our true motives. Is our faith genuine, or are we simply hoping for a windfall? Is Jesus our deliverer, or is he simply one option? Tough love from Jesus is often a discriminate tool for the masses that seek his intervention.

> Then Jesus answered, "Woman, you have great faith! Your request is granted." And her daughter was healed from that very hour.
>
> v. 28

She won him over, by golly. He resisted; she persisted. He pushed; she held. I don't think Jesus was being mean; I believe he was being shrewd. Would you throw money at any charity that called you? Would you invest in every "opportunity" presented to you? Of course not. You'd ask discerning questions; you'd play the devil's advocate. You'd press until your reservations were answered.

Praying for your child? Keep going. Persist. Stick with Jesus, even if his response seems concealed or delayed. Hang onto his ankles and let him know you're not moving. Stay the course and respond to the questions Jesus throws at you. Understand that sometimes his timing is linked to an examination of your heart, and hold steady. Keep going. Never give up.

See, there once was this mom who interceded for her child. . . .

○ Do you need to hang onto Jesus's ankles and beg for your child? What do you need?

○ If Jesus pressed on your motives, what would he find?

STEP OUT OF THE SPIN CYCLE

If you need to, be that persistent mama today. Make time to pray, to intercede, to never give up.

27

Vivienne

When we're talking to our girlfriends on the phone or spending glorious time with them sans kids, motherhood takes on a glossy veneer. We tell adorable stories; we recount their cute prayers or little comments. We might explain our latest discipline technique or new strategy. We speak in normal voices, and to all observers we are rational, reasonable women with a decent handle on parenting.

But sometimes when our kids are in tow, it becomes clear that we are actually raising miniature terrorists. There is something so horrifyingly embarrassing about your preschooler refusing to share, knocking kids down, insisting on his way, bossing God and everybody else. It feels like an indictment on what *really* goes on in your house, like you let your little insurgent run amok while you eat Pringles and watch *Days of Our Lives* all day. *Sure* you discipline.

It takes kids about five days to sprout the selfish gene. Anyone who says humans aren't born with a sinful nature has never been around a toddler. One of the hardest lessons to teach our little egotists is servanthood. Sharing, celebrating others' achievements, not being first, resisting competition . . . these are the battles of the young mind.

Here's a good story of when Jesus was invited to dinner at a bigwig's house:

> When he noticed how the guests picked the places of honor at the table, he told them this parable: "When someone invites you to a wedding feast, do not take the place of honor, for a person more distinguished than you may have been invited. If so, the host who invited both of you will come and say to you, 'Give this man your seat.' Then, humiliated, you will have to take the least important place."
>
> Luke 14:7–9

The hosts provided the food, the guests brought their egos, and Jesus brought the tension. Awesome. I'm sure they were mortified to be detected for their posturing. Positioning is something we all do, but we don't want to be noticed for it. (I had a similar moment when a friend was lamenting how bored her daughter was in school because her maturity level was through the roof—"She's head and shoulders above her peers!"—and if I were Jesus, I would've said, "When you talk about your daughter, don't act like a braggadocios loon. There are tons of kids smarter than your genius.")

Jesus teaches a lesson we would be wise to pass on to our children: someone is always going to be smarter, faster, funnier, and better than you. This is hard for our littles. They are hyper-aware of who can already write her name, who learned to ride a bike first, who was picked for line leader, who can do the middle splits. Early childhood feels like a developmental race to our children, and frankly, sharing feels like it is for suckers—be it toys, attention, or glory.

Teaching our kids intentional deference is essential. I taught my kids this story in Luke. I painted the picture of a woman who was totally over-made—big hat, bright clothes, mink coat—sashaying down the aisle and saying (in a high voice, I don't know why): "I'm sitting in the FRONT ROW, everyone! I'm a really big deal! Aren't you impressed? I would NEVER sit anywhere but the FRONT ROW! Everyone make room!" We named her Vivienne.

But then the mayor arrived, and the wedding planner escorted him to the front of the church and said to Vivienne, "Oh no, you're going to have to move. This is the MAYOR, for crying out loud! You need to take your fur coat and move to the back." So Vivienne endured the walk of shame in front of everyone who had heard her bragging. (Sydney: "I feel sorry for Vivienne." Gavin: "Sydney, you're so missing the point again.")

> But when you are invited, take the lowest place, so that when your host comes, he will say to you, "Friend, move up to a better place." Then you will be honored in the presence of all your fellow guests. For everyone who exalts himself will be humbled, and he who humbles himself will be exalted.
>
> Luke 14:10–11

Our kids have to learn to give up their front-row seat. They'll either learn to defer willingly or they'll be booted by the mayor for the rest of their lives, shocked at their true rank and swallowed by jealousy. When we train our children to take the lowest place, honor will find them through the back door of humility.

When my kids are positioning, insisting on their way, or taking stabs at someone else's success, we have a code word: Vivienne. It reminds them to give up their seat before this becomes a situation they'll regret. Interestingly, when they choose second place, their friends start doing the same. Giving honor is contagious.

Viva la Vivienne.

STEP OUT OF THE SPIN CYCLE

Make a really big deal today when your child defers in any way. Teach her this lesson, then give her a chance to try it out with you, a sibling, or a friend.

28

Our Own Little Sweatshop

Wisdom is proved right by all her children.

Luke 7:35

It's a confusing journey God puts moms on. We can barely be apart from our babies for twenty minutes at first. Eighteen years later, we're supposed to send them into the world as responsible and independent young adults. The timeline between those two is about eight hundred bottles of Advil, fifty books on parenting, and eight seasons of Dr. Phil DVDs.

Putting our kids' best interests first means accepting this fact: they'll live most of their lives outside our homes. We are either equipping them for success or stunting their growth, sometimes irreparably. Keeping our kids glued to our side cripples their ability to become independent.

Here's the trick: those muscles of responsibility must be exercised continuously, otherwise they atrophy and our kids won't stand on their own two feet when it's time. When we do everything for them, they never learn to do anything on their own. The real tragedy is they don't even know they can.

Expect this to go over with your kids like school on a Saturday.

Codependence is the bent of the immature heart. Kids push back when we push them toward responsibility. Most don't go willingly. In my house, it sounds like this: I can't do that. I'm too little. Will you do it? I don't know how. This is too hard. My arms are going to fall off. I don't like growing up. I wish I was a baby again.

Have older kids? It might sound more like this: I don't feel like doing that. I'm not a slave. We do all the work. This house sucks. I'm never making my kids do all this! My friends' parents pay for everything. (Or, later: Can I move back in?)

This process will look different depending on where you are on the timeline. Your two-year-old cannot make her own dinner, but if you're doing laundry for a sixteen-year-old, it's time for a Come to Jesus meeting. In our house, we live by two rules:

1. *What can you and should you be doing on your own?* I remember when my three kids (ages three, five, and seven then) brought their dirty clothes downstairs to the laundry room, turned their clothes right side out, and separated them into piles by color. Their heads barely reached the top of the washing machine. My husband said, "It's like our own little sweatshop." Your kids can do more than *both* of you think. Regularly ask this question and reevaluate.

2. *Everyone is in charge of his or her own stuff.* This includes everything. Shoes, backpacks, dirty clothes, clutter, bedroom, bathroom stuff, papers, towels, dirty dishes, trash, clean clothes . . . it's not mama's problem. This includes my sweet husband. I was losing untold hours picking up things that didn't belong to me. We now have fifteen minutes of house recovery every night. If it belongs to you, take care of it.

These two rules have changed my life.

Cutting the apron strings doesn't just happen the day our kids go to college; it's the result of parenting them toward responsibility from birth. Jesus said, "Wisdom is proved right by all her children." We can all agree with that. Wisdom sends children out independent and mature, capable of critical thinking and cleaning a toilet.

Be encouraged by Jesus's words, girls. Wise parenting is hard on the front end and, consequently, is often plagued with uncertainty. The enemy will whisper doubt in your ear: She can't do that. He needs you. You're abandoning her if you won't step in. It's too much work. You're being too hard on them. She's too young.

Between the inevitable temper tantrums, the obstinacy, and the defiance, it's challenging to stay the course. Every mother knows it's easier to just do it yourself. It's easier not to administer consequences. It's easier to take the path of least resistance.

But "wisdom is proved right by all her children." Jesus knows the fruit comes later. Wisdom costs us at the front end but is proved in the long run. He parents us the same way. Jesus has wisely instructed me to do all kinds of things I didn't want to do, before I felt ready to do them:

Jesus	Me
"Write a book."	"I can't. I don't know how."
"Love homeless people."	"I'm scared to."
"Start a church."	"Can't someone else do it?"

Yet his wisdom was proved right in the end. These instructions changed me forever. He pushed me to obedience, and my entire life has been transformed. Jesus knew what he was talking about—and so do you, mom. Wise parenting—inconvenient, laborious, and relentless—will be confirmed later when you've turned selfish kids into healthy, dependable adults. Look at your children and see future husbands and next-generation mothers. Give them what they need to succeed: responsibility, initiative, and independence. Your future son- or daughter-in-law will thank you.

And those whiny kids who aren't your slaves? They'll thank you too.

○ If tethering your children to your side and perpetuating their dependence is a 1, and mothering them toward independence and cutting the apron strings is a 10, where do you fall on the scale? Why do you say that?

STEP OUT OF THE SPIN CYCLE

What are you currently doing that your children and husband should be doing for themselves? List everything and round everyone up. Time for a Come to Jesus meeting.

Upper Percentage
of the Average Rank

Gavin: Mom? You might not know this, but in fifth grade there is like a ranking system.

Me: Hmmm? (Encouraging him to go on, but LIKE I DON'T KNOW ABOUT THE RANKING SYSTEM. Fifth grade was my lowest-ranking year, no thanks to my home perm and bargain selection glasses. I bear residual scars to this day.)

Gavin: It's not written down or anything, but everyone just sort of knows.

Me: What's your rank, sweetie?

Gavin: I'm in the upper percentage of the average rank.

Me: (trying so very hard not to laugh) Tell me about that.

Gavin: Well, the top rank is like Braden and his
friends, and they're nice to me, but they
mostly stick with their own kind. I have a
bunch of friends in the low rank. The low and
average ranks merge a lot. There's less cross-
over between the average and top rank, and
the low rankers never get top rank time. It's
complicated, Mom.

Indeed.

Ranking systems, contests, competitions, tryouts, levels,
titles . . . the caste system is activated the first moment another baby is the first in the group to roll over. The hierarchy
is staffed, funded, organized, and maintained through the
diligent work of parents. The mommy competition should
have come as no surprise to me, but it did. The pressure I
felt to produce high-performing children who would breeze
through the top ranks of *everything* was staggering.

I asked my mom, "Did you and your friends have an un-
spoken competition through your kids? Did you feel a lot of
pressure?"

"No! That's ridiculous. That's something your crazy generation does. We just raised you. You and your friends *parent*." (Insert eye rolling.)

My memory confirms this statement. Our parents let us
try anything we wanted, even if we butchered the mechanics
or had no skill set whatsoever. Our dad then told us we were
terrific, and we didn't realize until adulthood that we were
the most average kids ever.

Girls, when are we going to realize that we are raising real
humans? Our children will struggle and fail and disappoint
us. I'm sorry to be the bearer of this news, but they will never
be the best at everything. Empty nesters totally get this; young
moms are still holding onto the dream. We're still controlling
and positioning and creating a failure-free environment.

Can you imagine how insecure our kids must feel?

When they are not allowed to fail, to bomb, to try something and only reach the average rank, we are branding them with unattainable perfection. In this society of "believe and achieve" rhetoric this will sound heretical, but in many, many ways, our kids are regular. I'm not advocating the dumbing down of America, and certainly our children shine brightly within their gifts, but sometimes she's just the unremarkable ballerina in the third row, second from the left.

You know how Jesus felt about performing and competing for attention. He was constantly pulling up the root of pride. Praying to be seen? You've received your reward in full. Giving for the sake of applause? No prize for you. Fasting to be noticed? Talk to the hand.

When Jesus reduced his kingdom to two rules, second only to "Love God" was "Love your neighbor as yourself" (see Matt. 22:36–40). As mothers, many of us love our children exactly like we "love" ourselves: critically. The standard of perfection by which we measure our own performance is automatically used on our kids. Don't imagine they don't pick up on it.

I taught first grade for a year and have mostly fond memories. ("Dear Mrs. Hatmaker, I love you as much as God. Love, Anjali.") One of my students was a cute-as-a-whippet girl named Madilyn. She was spunky and sparkly, and as a student, she was somewhere in the middle of the pack. Of course, her parents immediately signed her up for gifted testing, and her scores came back too low for the label. They immediately called a meeting with me and my principal and begged, "What can we do to make her gifted?!"

That poor girl. She's sixteen now, and I bet she's been through the wringer trying to "become gifted" to make her parents happy.

Let's not perpetuate this trend. I want to create an environment where my kids are celebrated for their successes, but no one is going to die if they fail—or even worse, just end up in the middle of the pack. Let them try new things, risk free. Allow them to stick with something just for the love of it, even if they'll never win a college scholarship. Let's teach them what to do with failure: talk about it, evaluate it, learn from it, and get over it. And if it turns out that my superstar only makes it to the upper percentage of the average rank?

No worries. He's still the cutest kid in middle school history (wink).

○ Are you a perfectionist mom? If so, what do you do to reach the top rank? (How do you parent? How do you talk to your friends about your kids?)

STEP OUT OF THE SPIN CYCLE

Try to relax today. Attempt to be non-controlling. See if the whole house exhales with relief.

30

Working Girls

My girlfriend Trina and her daughter, Hannah, were discussing her future. Now Hannah is a skilled button-pusher when it comes to her mom. So, understanding Trina's active professional life and how deeply she values education and career, Hannah knew just what to say when Trina asked her about college:

"I'm not going to college. I'll just get married and have babies."

Even knowing that Hannah was manipulating her into overreaction, Trina still did it. "What? That is ridiculous! You are no more going to get married without going to college than I'm going to go to church without a bra on! You can forget that! And if you engineer a wedding when you're eighteen years old, then you'll know just where to find me. I'll be the drunk mother-of-the-bride passed out on the dance floor! Just step over me and dance your way into a life of disappointment and regret!"

Hannah couldn't have been more pleased with her mother's reaction, even if I've embellished it just a tad.

Now Hannah was nine at the time, so I'm not sure we had a bona fide crisis on our hands just yet, but we dream about our children's futures like we dreamed of our own, do we not? God created us for work. Solomon told us that our "appetite is an incentive to work; hunger makes you work all the harder" (Prov. 16:26 Message). Who created that appetite within us? God gives us a hunger for our passion; a physical need to discover our work. He blesses us with gifts for application, zeal for fuel, conviction for direction, and intelligence for success. Focused work is God's idea, and he equips us individually for it.

Here's what I want to say about this: there is no biblical prototype for what a "working woman" looks like. Nowhere does it say we must only be housewives. Nowhere does it say we must be employed full-time. In fact, there are women in Scripture at both ends of the work spectrum and in the middle. God led them all to their work capacity.

If you judge other moms who work differently than you, stop it right now. Concluding that other women's work should look like yours is like saying everyone should favor lasagna because you do. I mean, lasagna is delicious, but some girls just prefer fish. Some girls don't have any choice. We have diverse callings, families, circumstances, and goals that God alone knows how to manage. We're turning on our teammates when we draw these dividing lines. We're all serving the same coach, and as Paul reminded us: "Who are you to judge someone else's servant? To his own master he stands or falls. *And he will stand, for the Lord is able to make him stand*" (Rom. 14:4, emphasis added).

Jesus put it rather unambiguously: "Do not judge" (see Matt. 7:1).

Can you imagine how much heartache would be avoided if we obeyed Jesus in this one command? Do you realize how much carnage he tried to spare us from by telling us not to judge each other? Wars would be averted. Marriages would be saved. Tribes would have peace. Races would find reconciliation. Our churches would be jam-packed. And mothers would be delivered from the horrible guilt trips we send each other on.

I was booked for an event in Memphis last year, and a few days before I flew out, a package was delivered. Inside was a "weekend survival kit" for my family: popcorn, DVDs, hot chocolate, a board game, and books. My event planner attached a note:

> Dear Brandon, Gavin, Sydney, and Caleb: Thank you so much for the gift of your mom this weekend! We are so grateful that you are lending her to us to teach us the Word and encourage us in our faith. You should be so proud to have a mom who uses her gifts. Enjoy the goodies and we'll send her back to you on Saturday!

I have never been so encouraged for my work choice in my life. Not the tilted head of pity: "Oh? You travel for your job? I'm sorry." Not the slightly veiled criticism: "Must be hard for your family." Not the opposite pressure to become the next Beth Moore: "You could be doing so much more." That sweet girl loved on my family and affirmed my calling to my children. (You love on me? Nice. You love my babies? We are BFFs forever.)

Some women have to work, some women want to work, some women work at home—and that's okay! It's all in the same bucket, and it's all valuable. Jesus gives you much grace for your role, so we should extend the same grace to each other. The question isn't, "Right or wrong?" The question should be, "Healthy or not?" None of us has the authority or perspective to make that call for another mom. God leads each of us in wisdom, and "work" can look a thousand different ways. He alone completely understands your family, your circumstances, your gifts, and your season of life, so he alone gets to direct the path you take.

Exhale. God values you and the very hard work you do every day.

Make sure your work is working—and that assessment is between you, your family, and God. The rest of us can butt out and quit criticizing your choices until we have walked a day in your shoes.

(*Jen gets down off soapbox.*)

○ How is your work working for you, whether in the home or out of the home?

○ If you could make any adjustment, what would it be? What stops you from taking that plunge?

STEP OUT OF THE SPIN CYCLE

If you had an answer for the above question, take one tangible step toward that goal. Initiate a conversation, make an adjustment, or make the first move.

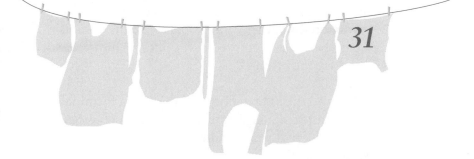

Those Are the Prunes

Every mom has a stack of books she's read to her children so many times that she could close her eyes and recite every page by memory. With these, you can't get away with turning four pages at once or skipping entire paragraphs . . . not that I've ever done that. Our family had several hall of famers: the Carl series, *Alligator Baby*, *One Fish Two Fish Red Fish Blue Fish*, and all books by Shel Silverstein. (Just last week, Sydney called Caleb into her room to "do devotionals together," and when I peeked in on this preciousness fifteen minutes later, they were reading their favorite poems from *Falling Up* to each other. Well, it's a start.)

Anyhow, one book we read endlessly was *Everywhere Babies*, which made me choke up while reading about every one in three times. Each page discussed one element of babyhood, in all its diversity. One said:

Every day, everywhere, babies are fed—by bottle, by breast, with cups, and with spoons, with milk and cereal, carrots, and prunes.[4]

Little pencil drawings illustrated each feeding option, and Gavin—probably five at the time—unexposed to the term and taking his best guess, pointed to the nursing mother and said, "Those are the prunes."

Touché.

Childbirth and the human body combine as a formidable team, with definite collateral damage. When Caleb recently sauntered into the bathroom while I was getting ready and asked, "What are all those scratches on your stomach, Mom?" he was permanently uninvited from the bathroom scene.

I don't mean to shock you, doves, but our bodies change after childbirth. They really, really change. I sprouted curls in previously stick-straight hair, and my feet grew an entire shoe size by the third baby. I now walk around on skis. My hips have never returned exactly to their former address. I nursed three babies and need not mention what a mess that left. What used to be a smooth stomach now looks like a topographical map of France. And to top it all off, I can't jump on trampolines anymore without peeing in my pants.

Traditional Christian advice about this subject generally makes me feel violent. People, I am not standing naked in front of the mirror, quoting Scripture to my reflection. If this approach works for you, then by all means carry on. But it comes up short for me. It's like looking at a garden salad with fat-free dressing and saying, "I love you. I am thrilled to be eating you instead of a delicious burger with a side of beer-battered onion rings."

Because here is the deal: it is okay to be a little bummed out by your stretch marks and saggy situation. If you tell me

---

4. Susan Meyers, *Everywhere Babies* (New York: Scholastic Printing, 2002).

you adore your new hypersensitive bladder and adult acne, I'm going to call you a liar and unfriend you on Facebook. Some of the bodily changes that come with childbirth stink, and I'm giving you permission to feel that way.

That said, I'm going back to something Jesus taught.

> Therefore I tell you, do not worry about your life, what you will eat; or about your body, what you will wear. Life is more than food, and the body more than clothes.
>
> Luke 12:22–23

Your body is more than clothes; it is also more than loose skin and bigger feet. Our bodies nourished babies and brought them into this world. (I'd like to see one man endure this—the human race would be extinct.) Our bodies run through our husbands' minds twenty times a day, wider hips notwithstanding. Our bodies deserve a prize for enduring the marathon of early childhood: lifting, carrying, bending, squatting, wrestling, holding, lugging, running, chasing, pushing, and rocking.

Our bodies have allowed us to experience the intimacy of marriage and the marvels of motherhood. They gave us a backstage pass to wonders like nursing and childbirth. They've worked hard, our bodies, and they deserve a little love.

My girlfriend heard a sermon by a husband-and-wife team on marriage, and the wife stated in front of thousands of people and a television audience: "If you weigh more than ten pounds over your wedding day weight, you need to go on a diet." I'm sure there were multiple hits taken out on her life.

Girls, we don't need to be within ten pounds of our pre-baby, twenty-something weight, but every woman knows she feels better when she is taking care of her body. Taking care means we are feeding our body food that will nourish it and protecting it from destructive habits. It means we care about *health*. My 93-year-old grandma, whose body is broken and collapsing from the inside-out, told me sadly: "If I'd known

I was going to live this long, I would've taken much better care of myself."

This is my one and only body. This is the skin I will still be living in forty years from now. This heart is the one I'll be counting on; these hands are the same ones I'll use to hold grandbabies. It doesn't look the same as it did fifteen years ago, but that body was young and untested. This body, the one I'm living in now, is responsible for three beautiful children who now occupy this planet. It carried them, birthed them, and still had enough left over to raise them. I'm proud of it, even if I don't love all its aesthetics.

Your body is more than clothes. It is your friend and ally. It is the vessel that will carry you for the rest of your days, until you shed it for your permanent glory. In the meantime, treat it with the respect it deserves and the attention it requires. Granted, it's given you a boob situation you didn't ask for, but you once fed it Sonic for eight straight days after the restaurant's grand opening just up the street (oops). Let's call it even and declare a ceasefire.

Peace.

○ What does your inner critic say about your body?

STEP OUT OF THE SPIN CYCLE

Write down five ways your body has served you well.

32

Dogs and Discipleship

The Hatmakers have false-started several times on dog ownership. There are a myriad of reasons for this, like realizing dogs take work, for example. We let our impulsive tendencies prevail when staring at a puppy in the back of someone's truck or in front of PetSmart. The puppies' faces seem to say, "Own me. I am a living Hallmark moment. I shall frolic with you and bring joy and meaning to your family." The children's faces conspire with them: "We need this puppy. We will spend every second with him. We will walk and feed and poop-scoop with joy. You'll never even realize we have a dog because we will be so responsible for all his needs."

Buy dog.

Realize aforementioned kids are liars.

Scrub pee-pee carpet.

Throw chewed shoes (toys, remote controls, cups, everything) into trash.

Find new home for dog.

The kids didn't care for this pattern (and who could blame them?). We were lame pet owners who have since been reformed and now own a trained and beloved springer spaniel. But before our rehabilitation, we went three years without a pet while our kids ran down every dog they saw for a petting, while telling perfect strangers their parents gave away all their dogs and refused to buy another one. Lovely.

Then this piece of scholarship came home from Gavin, entitled *Heartbreak*: "The saddest moment of my life was when my mom gave our dogs away. She was sick of them because they were too crazy. But I forgave my mom. She's all right. At least she's not dead." Why his dad wasn't also indicted for this I have no idea, but evidently I've been forgiven and things could clearly be worse: I could be in the morgue.

> Suppose one of you wants to build a tower. Will he not first sit down and estimate the cost to see if he has enough money to complete it? For if he lays the foundation and is not able to finish it, everyone who sees it will ridicule him, saying, "This fellow began to build and was not able to finish." . . . In the same way, any of you who does not give up everything he has cannot be my disciple.
>
> Luke 14:28–30, 33

Jesus knew how to thin out a crowd, yes? I like this side of Jesus. He never sugarcoated faith or made discipleship sound easy. I've grown weary of the prosperity gospel and a generation of believers turning to Jesus for what he can give them. There is no substance to a faith that sticks only when the sun is shining.

But let's be honest: this is a hard teaching. Did Jesus really mean it? If we don't give up everything, we can't be his disciples? *Everything?* Jesus basically warned, "Consider the cost and don't start what you can't finish." This makes more sense to me the longer I live. I'm at least beginning to get my head around the price of true discipleship.

Here is what I'm finding: I struggle infinitely more with giving up emotional and spiritual control than with giving up tangible possessions. I easily give the shoes off my feet, but letting go of my pride is a constant battle. We've gladly given money, time, and assistance, but releasing my need for approval is a sacrifice I still struggle to offer.

As mothers, giving up control over our children is as difficult as starting the Atkins diet in December. This is one area we do not trust Jesus to handle as well as we could. We tend to craft their destinies with careful planning and strategic positioning. We prefer safety and security—but if you've read even just five pages of the Bible, you know that's not God's priority. It's easier to commit our babies to Jesus in the season when their physical care falls entirely to us. It's much harder when our responsibilities lessen and God begins charting their life courses.

As disciples, as mothers, Jesus is telling us: "There is a cost to this. Will you be able to trust me with your children in five years? In ten years? Can you give up control? Will you trust me when they're struggling? When they fail? If I push them in a direction you're uncomfortable with? Can you give them to me *really*?"

Genuine trust in Jesus is revealed by what we are willing to trust him with, what we are prepared to give up for him and to him. The greater the treasure offered, the truer the faith, and of all that God has given us to steward, the hardest to release fully back to him is our children—more than our money, our possessions, or our gifts. It's a demonstration of the highest level of trust. It's building the tower to completion, knowing in advance you have saved enough to finish it.

This is something to nail down now, while you still have cribs and pull-up diapers in your home. You only have your children for a season, because truly, their lives belong to Christ. He has a mission for them that is outside your control and beyond your management. When they are tiny, and you are literally keeping them alive, this is the moment to say, "They belong to you, Jesus." Accept your task as it is. You are steadily working yourself out of a job and passing the baton to Jesus. The sooner you acknowledge the role you play, the easier it will be to release them, bit by bit, until they launch.

○ What does an eighteen-year-old look like whose entire life has been controlled and carefully manipulated by his mom?

○ If you believed Jesus was ultimately responsible for your children, what area or struggle would you release to him?

STEP OUT OF THE SPIN CYCLE

Spend a short time in prayer, asking God to develop your trust of his reign in your children's lives.

33

Professional Worrier

As I prepared to write a devotional about raising children with special needs, it dawned on me: I had no clue about raising a child with special needs. So I interviewed my friend Monica, who is raising two beautiful sons: Joshua, age nine, with autism, and Jacob, age eight, with dyslexia. Let her story encourage *any* of you raising a child who is atypical, different, challenging, or unique. Or perhaps you're one of those rare mothers who struggles with worry (sarcasm intended). If so, read on . . .

"How did your motherhood story start, Monica?"

All mothers have dreams, concerns, or worries that begin from the moment you discover you are pregnant. You begin to dream, and plan the future for your child and visualize appearance, sports, hobbies, career, marriage, etc. You don't, or at least I did not, insert the dream of a special need in your child's future. But the Lord did.

I will never forget the day I noticed something was different about my baby boy. Of course I began to compare him to my friends' babies, and then the worrying started to take hold of my thoughts—all of my thoughts, it consumed me. When the doctors confirmed my fears, I felt as though my legs were knocked out from under me and the breath was sucked out of my lungs. My child *was* different, and that meant everything would be different from this point forward!

That was the day I became a professional worrier. I worried about his developmental milestones, what he ate and when he ate it, which specialists to see and what therapies to sign up for, which children would/would not be appropriate to play with, and what other mothers would think of my ability to be a perfect mother. Let's face it: I worried about everything.

"How did you find your way through it?"

It wasn't until my precious baby was two years older that I realized he was happy every day, through all situations, all therapies, and all playdates-gone-wrong, and paid no attention to what he was eating; and yes, sometimes that included paper! My precious son was smiling and playing and enjoying his life while I sat next to him worrying, fretting, and wasting my energy on things I could not change.

As I walked aimlessly down this unknown pathway of special-needs parenting I began to feel very alone, but by the grace of our Lord wandered upon Matthew 6, verses 25–34. Wow, he wrote that for me. I was sure of it (and he wrote it for you too). I cling to two verses in particular:

"Who of you by worrying can add a single hour to his life? . . . Therefore do not worry about tomorrow, for tomorrow will worry about itself. Each day has enough trouble of its own" (Matt. 6:27, 34).

Throughout this passage the Lord himself says do not worry about life. I think this is where he would include an exclamation point! He means what he says. We are *not* to worry about our basic needs being met. Your heavenly Father tells you not to worry about what you eat, drink, or wear; the basic needs of life. The same can be said for the "special needs" of your precious child.

Jesus was specific about which of the littlest of needs we should not concern ourselves with. However, we should also see this passage as if he left blanks there for us to fill in. "Therefore do not worry about_____." Fill this in with the special needs of your child: the doctor visits, therapies, medications, education, and health. We did not choose this path for our children, but the Lord did. God knows your fears, concerns, and worries, even if you do not speak them. Rest assured he can do a far better job of managing things than you can. Fix your eyes upon the Lord and give him the day that is before you. We are far more productive for our children when we seek his plan for our lives, and our child's life.

"What would you tell another mom of a child with special needs?"

As your child grew in your womb, God himself knit in unique threads of creativity, and we should embrace the fact that our child is *not* like everybody else. I consider it an honor that the Lord chose me to receive this very special gift that is truly like no other. I know that the Lord will supply me with exactly what I need to be the best mom I can be for my son. I love to see the glimmer in my boy's eyes when I say, "You are truly special." Then he smiles and I am blessed to know that "special" has more meanings than I ever knew.

I am blessed!

As for my worry, well, I am a recovering worry addict! It is not my primary focus, though it sneaks up on me at times, and that is when I run to my Father and cast all my cares upon him. Besides, I have too much to do today to worry about _____ (fill in the blank)!

○ If you have a child with any kind of special needs, what do you worry about the most?

STEP OUT OF THE SPIN CYCLE

While you're worrying, what charms are your son or daughter bringing to the world? List them all. Share that list with your family.

34

I'm Bringing Sexy Back

Listen: I love Jesus. I'm one of his biggest fans. When I don't know how to talk to someone about Christianity or church or Scripture or prophecy, I can always talk about Jesus, and they are guaranteed to love him. He is his own best advocate. I'm totally into his style and I dig his cool stories. Mine eyes have seen the glory of the coming of the Lord and stuff.

But let me tell you something: that guy did not have much to say on the topics of child raising, marriage, or—as it applies to this devotional—sex. Seriously. Mum was the word. Brandon stared at me last night while I was growling at my Bible, and I barked, "Jesus, couldn't you have worked in one good paragraph about motherhood? One tiny little piece of advice about keeping the fires burning with a toddler lying between you five nights a week?"

Alas, for this one devotional, we're deviating from Jesus and turning to Paul, who had much more to say on the subject. First Corinthians 7 starts out like this: "Now for the matters you wrote about," and an entire chapter on sex and marriage commences. This has been a hot topic forever. Jesus and his buds maybe didn't care so much, but everyone else sure did. The Corinthian church must've written a letter, gotten the obligatory spiritual stuff out of the way, and finally got around to the real issue: "So Paul, the men in our church want more sex than they're getting . . ." and thus we have this bit of advice for the ages:

> The husband should fulfill his marital duty to his wife, and likewise the wife to her husband. The wife's body does not belong to her alone but also to her husband. In the same way, the husband's body does not belong to him alone but also to his wife. Do not deprive each other except by mutual consent and for a time, so that you may devote yourselves to prayer. Then come together again so that Satan will not tempt you because of your lack of self-control.
>
> 1 Corinthians 7:3–5

Sex. Out of everyone I know, only about three couples have this issue sewn up. Men and women approach sex differently, think about it differently, need it differently, assess it differently. Yet we can only get it through each other. But God does not set us up for failure. So what was he thinking?

Think about the other facets of marriage God loves: affection, mutuality, respect, and commitment. Girls, when those are flourishing, sex follows more naturally. God didn't drop us in the marriage pool and shout, "Spawn!" He placed the treasure of sex within marriage, fiercely guarded by emotional togetherness. When those layers are broken or absent, sex is vulnerable, void of the context in which it thrives.

That's how women see it.

Men see it reversed. When sex is broken or absent, the relationship is vulnerable, void of the sexual togetherness that allows it to thrive. Sheila Gregoire put it like this: "She makes love *because* she feels loved, and he makes love *to* feel loved. In other words, when she doesn't feel loved, the last thing she wants is to make love. But when he feels distant, the thing he wants most is to make love because that's how he fixes everything."[5] Oh, dear.

"Do not deprive each other," cautioned Paul. But this does not mean a rolled-eye, deep-sigh "oh whatever, just get on with it" response to our husband's requests.

Who cares? Men just want sex, right? They don't care if we're into it. In Shaunti Feldhahn's survey in *For Women Only*, this topic earned the highest degree of unanimity: 97 percent of men said getting enough sex wasn't enough. Sheer quantity was not their desire. Rather, they needed to feel wanted. In fact, three out of four men said even if they were getting *all the sex they wanted*, they'd still feel empty if their wife wasn't both engaged and satisfied.[6]

Girls, we are relational creatures. We get emotional support from many sources. Most men live with a deep loneliness we don't understand. Often he stands alone—in the workplace, as a provider, or simply as a man, independent and strong. For him, sex is the purest salve for that loneliness. In your arms he is accepted, desired, loved. When he knows you want him sexually, you are emotionally arming him to succeed everywhere else.

I know what you're thinking: You've got to be kidding me. I'm exhausted. I've met needs since 6:00 a.m. If one more person gropes me, I'm getting the gun. I know that look and you can forget it.

Girls, I know! Lord have mercy, I understand. The idea of sex at 10:30 p.m. is so obnoxious sometimes, it makes us want to cry.

Sweet friends, remember: sex is not just sex to him. There is no stronger way to communicate your love than through your sexual desire. Inversely, there's no quicker way to verify his unworthiness than to reject him sexually. There is a tender

---

5. Sheila Wray Gregoire, *To Love, Honor, and Vacuum* (Grand Rapids: Kregel, 2003), 183.

6. Shaunti Feldhahn, *For Women Only* (Sisters, OR: Multnomah, 2004), 93–94.

heart behind that testosterone, no matter how much you may think otherwise.

One husband said, "When she says no, I feel that I am REJECTED. 'No' is not no to sex—as she might feel. It is no to me as I am. And I am vulnerable as I ask or initiate. It's plain and simple rejection."[7] Our husbands find us irresistible; they think about sex with us literally every hour. So when they feel unappealing to us, we don't understand how deep that cuts. You're thinking: *I'm just tired*. But he's hearing: *She doesn't want me*.

Girls, we want the emotional elements of marriage in place before dealing with this one. But it's only when sex is healthy that our husbands can meet our other needs. If all areas are dry, someone needs to be the hero. Yes, it's fair to feel entitled to mutuality and affection from him. But crippling his sexual needs will never produce the kind of marriage you're dreaming of. Do you want to be right, or do you want to be happy?

It's your turn to be the hero. Run headlong into the intoxicating power of sex. Allow God to work supernaturally as you join physically with your husband. Let the Spirit use your gift to minister to your partner's heart, and you might be shocked how it changes your entire union.

○ Are you struggling with sexual tension in your marriage? How so?

STEP OUT OF THE SPIN CYCLE

Sex fixes things for your man, which ultimately helps fix things for you. Initiate tonight. Let your partner know he is wanted. Treat him like he's first place.

---

7. Ibid., 100.

Mother of the Year Award

I realize I've mentioned my son Caleb many times already, but that kid is a wealth of material. He popped out exactly like he is, I assure you. I should've known I was in for it when, at thirteen months old, he was supposed to be napping. While I cleaned out my closet, evidently he crawled out of his crib (first time), crawled down the stairs, put Gavin's shoes on (the correct feet), opened the front door (new skill), crossed the street, unlatched my neighbor's gate (no, I am not kidding), crawled onto their trampoline, and had an afternoon jump.

When the doorbell rang, I came downstairs to find a strange woman on my porch, and my door was open. I thought, *What the heck? Did this woman open my door?* So I was unprepared for her question:

"Do you have a little blond boy?"

First thought: Gavin, five at the time—*He hit her kid. He stole her rain boots. He peed in her yard. He rode through her flowers.*

"Gavin? My five-year-old?"

"No, younger."

Bad feeling coming on. Dawning panic.

"There is a little boy stuck on Heather and Judd's trampoline, crying his eyes out. He's stuck. He's been there for fifteen minutes. I called them but they're not home. Is he yours? I saw your open door."

I raced down the street like FloJo and rescued my very hot, very distressed *thirteen month old* from the jaws of utter disaster. I obsessed over the what-ifs: a speeding car, a rabid dog, a murderer, a black market child dealer. We were one click away from becoming a *Dateline* story. I cried for three days and didn't put Caleb down for a week.

It's my first-place Horrible Mom Moment. (Other finalists include two-year-old Gavin briefly underwater while I talked to my friends at the pool, three-year-old Sydney lost in Dillards for twenty minutes, and the time Gavin and his best friend walked through the forest behind our house to Austin Community College, half a mile away, and called me from the lobby.)

> Every year his parents went to Jerusalem for the Feast of the Passover. When he was twelve years old, they went up to the Feast, according to the custom. After the Feast was over, while his parents were returning home, the boy Jesus stayed behind in Jerusalem, but they were unaware of it. Thinking he was in their company, they traveled on for a day. Then they began looking for him among their relatives and friends. When they did not find him, they went back to Jerusalem to look for him.
>
> After three days they found him in the temple courts, sitting among the teachers, listening to them and asking them questions. Everyone who heard him was amazed at his understanding and his answers. When his parents saw him, they were astonished.
>
> His mother said to him, "Son, why have you treated us like this? Your father and I have been anxiously searching for you."

"Why were you searching for me?" he asked. "Didn't you know I had to be in my Father's house?" But they did not understand what he was saying to them.

Luke 2:41–50

My son crossed the street alone, but hey: Mary lost the savior of the universe.

I'm sure losing your firstborn for three days was no motherhood picnic. I like Luke's simplified account of Mary's response: "Son, why have you treated us like this? Your father and I have been anxiously searching for you."

Any mom can envision her wild eyes, her "I-love-you-I'll-kill-you" reaction, her panic and horror. I imagine Mary back in Nazareth, sitting with her girlfriends, saying, "You guys are not going to BELIEVE what I did. I traveled a whole day before I even realized that kid was missing! Mother of the Year Award!"

Every mom since the beginning of time has had a Horrible Mom Moment. Get a group of honest women in a room and start asking; you'll see. We've left our kids at church. We lost it in the middle of Target. We crammed their feet in shoes they had outgrown and wondered why they were bawling all day. We let them cry it out in the middle of the night only to discover they were lying in puke. We dressed our sons in knickers (which should definitely count as some sort of abuse).

Horrible Mom Moments happen to mothers who are diligent, careful, loving, and attentive. They happen to mamas who are smart, cautious, watchful, and intentional. No one is immune. It's okay. Relax. We've all been there. If you haven't, just parent longer.

"But his mother treasured all these things in her heart" (v. 51). I imagine Mary bundled up the whole week—the trip, the debacle, the weird discovery of Jesus in the temple, the relief—and thought, "That's my kid, God love him! God help me!" (Literally.)

153

Horrible Mom Moments are part and parcel of this role. They are not reasons to doubt your ability to raise another human or to obsess over your mistakes. They shouldn't keep us sidelined in fear or paralyzed with anxiety. They're normal and common, and we're going to have a million before our kids are grown. They are part of the crazy, unpredictable, extreme treasure trove that is motherhood. And hey, there is always a silver lining. . . .

They might sell a lot of books for you one day (wink).

○ What is your worst Horrible Mom Moment?

STEP OUT OF THE SPIN CYCLE

Allow that moment to lose some of its power over you. Tell someone. Ask about hers. Laugh it off or shake it off together.

36

No Loving in First Grade

Like it or not, our youngest son Caleb is something of a Casanova. The ladies love him. He's managed to perfect the male swagger at age seven. This is going to be terribly alarming in ten years, but for now, his animal magnetism is moderately entertaining. When Sydney gets off the bus and yells, "Kimberly kissed Caleb without even asking him!" Caleb shrugs his shoulders and rolls his eyes, like, "Women. What are you going to do?"

In first grade, Caleb dropped his backpack dramatically in our front hall and sighed. "Mom? Brooke, Tatum, Skylar, and Kate all want me to be their boyfriend. I told Mrs. Taylor and she said, 'No loving in first grade.'" (Other truisms Mrs. Taylor was forced to say that year to my son: "Kissing is for families." "No, sarcasm is *not* a sin. How do you think your mom makes a living?" "Put the deer horns on my desk for the rest of the day." "You cannot punch Cole for calling you Caleb Buttmaker." God bless her.)

In the season of first grade, loving wasn't in the option pool.

May I tell you something, mom? Something you need to hear and I'm dying to tell you? During this short period of raising little ones, you have permission to remove a legion of activities from your option pool. This is the optimal time to say "no," "not yet," "I can't," and "maybe in three years."

I volunteered to lead a Bible study during this season, and I cannot remember a single spiritual truth I learned the entire year. Here's what I remember: pulling my babies out of bed early in order to get them changed, dressed, fed, and packed in time to get to church. I remember wrangling them into the car, running one back in for a diaper change when he had a blowout, getting three miles down the road before realizing I left the baby's bottle in the refrigerator, speeding back home because even I was not cruel enough to unload that kind of disaster on the nursery workers, driving fifteen miles over the speed limit to get to church because now I was late, running in with three children, diaper bags, snack baggies, and Bible study paraphernalia dangling from all parts of my body, throwing these three small humans into childcare with apologies ("I couldn't find Sydney's pacifier. I am so sorry. I'll write you a check for $1000 for your pain and suffering when I pick her up."), skidding into Bible study with two minutes to spare, greeting my group and trying desperately to remember what the study was even about, and struggling to think about God stuff when all I wanted to do was take a nap.

The chaos of wrangling my littles to a morning Bible study completely negated any and all positive effects for me. By the time I got there, I was frazzled, stressed, and wondering why on earth I had agreed to it. What is now an utter delight to me was a grueling task then—one I resented and regretted.

Jesus had a total grasp on the concept of timing. He knew when to say "yes" and when to say "no," and when to say "not yet." He wouldn't be pushed into anything too soon, distracted from his current mission, or taken away from his task. He said things like:

- "My appointed time is near" (Matt. 26:18).
- "The time will come when not one stone will be left on another" (Luke 21:6).
- "My time has not yet come" (John 2:4).
- "The right time for me has not yet come" (John 7:6).
- "I am with you for only a short time" (John 7:33).

Each season of Jesus's life had a specific purpose, and he drew tight boundaries around his mission. He didn't go public before he was ready, he didn't perform miracles before he selected disciples, he wouldn't commission them until they'd apprenticed, he didn't lay down his life until the appointed time. Jesus was patient, focused, and never said "yes" until the timing was right.

You are in a season, dear friend, and it will not last forever. You have permission to draw tight boundaries around your mission. You can say "no" to all kinds of busyness—in church and in your community. You can say "no" to Christmas at your parents' house two states away. They can come to you while you have young children. You can say "no" to some of the marvelous things you did with excellence before children—you might have organized the best silent auction ever, but now you have a baby and a toddler, and either your fundraiser would be toast or you'd have to abandon your children for a month to pull it off. You can say "no" to the greeter ministry at church. You can say "no" to the PTA.

You can say "no."

This is the season to say "yes" to very specific things. "Yes" to a simple schedule that doesn't mutilate the rhythm of your household. "Yes" to activities that make sense for everyone. "Yes" to your sanity. "Yes" to your husband and precious time at home with your whole family. "Yes" to a realistic workload.

"Yes" to your children, who will soon outgrow this stage while you return to your regularly scheduled program.

Like Jesus understood, "I am with you for only a short time."

○ Have you said "yes" to too many things? What needs to go?

○ If you're worried about "letting someone down" or "being selfish," answer this: how are these activities affecting your life and the rhythm of your home?

STEP OUT OF THE SPIN CYCLE

If you need to, take the first step today toward healthier boundaries. Send an email. Make a phone call. Find a replacement. Say "no."

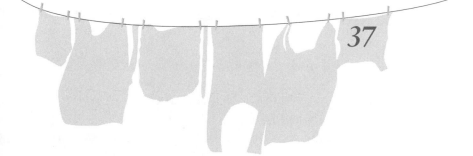

Do What the Voices Say

All three of our kids have asked Jesus to save them from their own junk, and Brandon has baptized them all. It's interesting to observe the presence of the Holy Spirit in their lives. Certainly, their faith is young and undeveloped, but Jesus said he resides in the hearts of believers, and there is no age requirement for that indwelling.

Consequently, they have shared various moments of "hearing from God" with us. This is how God talks to my children:

Gavin: "Mom? I've been thinking about the kingdom of God. I learned that it's not just later, but the Bible said 'it's near.' God is showing me how to help his kingdom come now in my life. Do you know what I mean?"

Sydney: "Mom? When I was praying last night, I changed from the things I normally ask about, because I felt like God wanted me to pray for that homeless woman we met last time who only had on little shorts and a tank top. It was so cold last night that I just felt like I should pray for her to be warm and safe."

Caleb: "Mom? Do you only hear one voice in your head? Because I hear millions."

Me: "Umm. What do you mean, honey? What kind of voices?"

Caleb: "Well, now that I'm a Christian, you know I can hear God."

Me: "Okay. Yes. True. So what is God saying to you?"

Caleb: "Mostly he just says . . . 'No.'"

All this sounds spot on. These are exactly the sorts of things I'd expect God to be telling each individual kid I birthed. It's a good thing Caleb is a Christian, because he needs several voices in his head telling him "no." (Thank you, God, Jesus, and the Holy Spirit, for helping me parent him. It takes a village.)

Jesus explained:

> The watchman opens the gate for him, and the sheep listen to his voice. He calls his own sheep by name and leads them out. When he has brought out all his own, he goes on ahead of them, and his sheep follow him because they know his voice.
>
> John 10:3–4

Any first century listener would've recognized the nuances of a shepherd calling his sheep. A shepherd was intimately acquainted with every single sheep in his flock. He knew their habits, their personalities, and their tendencies. In fact, he developed a specific call for each sheep. A shepherd could stand outside the flock and make a particular call, and that one sheep would separate from the flock and come to him. Every sheep had its own special language with the shepherd.

Mama, you are shepherding your little flock, and each of your tiny sheep is different. Their personalities require a certain brand of communication. Some children need gentleness and subtlety. Others need directness and brevity. Certain kids require lots of attention while others need alone time. Some children like everything explained in detail, but others can only handle a one-sentence explanation before glazing over.

My first sheep is a minimalist—keep the words few and the concepts simple, or be prepared for glassy eyes. His quality time simply involves proximity, not communication. My second sheep has two million questions about every detail of every situation of every possibility in the universe. She needs time, and lots of it. Don't skimp on the facts and don't you dare try to leave something out. My littlest lamb thrives on encouragement and does not respond to sarcasm *at all* (Houston, we have a problem).

I have to speak to each member of my flock in the language he or she is fluent in, or we are going to encounter a massive communication breakdown. I know what they need and what they can't handle. I know how to get their attention and how to keep it. If I force a call that doesn't fit my sheep, they are going to have a much harder time following me.

"The sheep listen to his voice. He calls his own sheep by name and leads them out." Learn to speak the language of your little flock, mom, just like Jesus does with us. Pay attention to what works and study their responses. Do the patient, loving work of distinguishing the needs of each child and meeting those needs uniquely. You may have to become fluent in several different languages, but your sheep will follow you when they hear their call.

○ How would you describe "the call" necessary for each of your children?

○ Have you been trying to push a square peg into a round hole with one of them? If so, what does that child need from you to improve communication?

STEP OUT OF THE SPIN CYCLE

Create a moment today to speak their exact love language to each of your children.

No Hands, No Jesus

My girlfriend Christi is raising a daughter her husband Brett calls "wild stallion," although her real name is Macy Caroline. She popped out sassy and spunky, that one. Christi has entertained us for years with stories, but one of my favorites happened when Macy Caroline was just 22 months old.

The three of them sat down to dinner, and Christi—ever the discipling mother—said, "Okay, MC. Let's all hold hands and pray to Jesus before we eat." And as she reached toward her, Macy Caroline jerked her hand away and deadpanned: "No hands."

Remaining patient, Christi restated, "Okay, we're just going to thank Jesus for our food before we eat it. You, me, and Daddy are going to pray together."

MC lowered her head and muttered, "No Jesus."

"We're praying before we eat, Macy Caroline, so you can choose. If you're not going to pray, then you're not going to eat."

After just one moment of hesitation, MC threw every ounce of her food on the ground and stared down her parents like a junior member of the mafia.

Into time-out she went, while Christi and Brett started eating. About every two minutes, Christi would ask, "Are you ready to come pray and eat with us?" And Macy Caroline would say:

"No hands, no Jesus."

Two minutes later: "Are you ready to make a good choice?"

"No hands, no Jesus."

Twenty-five minutes later, with the meal finished: "Macy Caroline? Are you ready now?"

"No hands, no Jesus."

Most not-quite-two-year-olds would have totally caved. Three minutes, tops, and they'd be praying to SpongeBob or whoever to get their chicken nuggets. But you know what they say: it's hard to break a wild stallion. . . .

Disciplining toddlers and preschoolers is like every mother's personal, daily Armageddon. When we held our innocent babies, who knew we'd encounter a will of iron just fifteen months later? Who knew they could dig their heels in and die on every hill? No one told us we'd put our children in time-out thirteen times in one day *for the same offense*. The obstinacy of a two-year-old can make a grown woman weep.

Look no further than the way God disciplines us to find encouragement. He is a parent too, and we are his wayward children. We've stomped our feet and thrown our food on the floor and said, "No _____, no Jesus." Here's how God handles our rebellion:

> "The Lord disciplines those he loves, and he punishes everyone he accepts as a son." Endure hardship as discipline; God is treating you as sons. For what son is not disciplined by his father?
>
> Hebrews 12:6–7

True love disciplines. It's just that simple. The highest form of love is to train our children while their own human nature is battling for control. Discipline recognizes that stubbornness turns into rebellion and disrespect turns into hostility. We simply love our children too much to let their enemy have his way with them—and yes, they have an enemy whose mission is to steal their innocence, kill their sweetness, and destroy their futures. Love compels us to intervene; it refuses to stand idly by, too tired to set limits or too passive to administer consequences.

> Moreover, we have all had human fathers who disciplined us and we respected them for it. How much more should we submit to the Father of our spirits and live!
>
> v. 9

This is a long-term investment, girls. Expect your children to resist the refining process now. Be prepared for tears, tantrums, and repeat offenders. A preschooler cannot think holistically about his own development or imagine himself in ten years—only you can do that, and you'll bear the burden of that foreknowledge. However, your child will one day respect you for the discipline you refused to neglect. When he is self-controlled, responsible, and trustworthy, he'll have you to thank. And he will. And so will his wife, boss, friends, neighbors, children, coworkers, and in-laws.

> No discipline seems pleasant at the time, but painful. Later on, however, it produces a harvest of righteousness and peace for those who have been trained by it.
>
> v. 11

Unpleasant and painful does not mean manic and hostile. Our children are humans and deserve to be treated respectfully. Discipline doesn't include raging, screaming, abusing, neglecting, humiliating, or shaming our kids. God never treats us like that. That sort of discipline never "produces a harvest of righteousness and peace."

Discipline means high standards—disrespect and disobedience are deal breakers in our house—and consistent consequences administered by a calm mother who is not acting like a candidate for the mental ward. Send your young deviant to her room for a couple of minutes while you calm down. Take deep breaths. Shed the anger. Identify the root you are pulling up from the soil of your child's heart: selfishness, defiance, aggression. When you're ready, speak calmly to her about your task as a mother, how God trusts you to train her. Discuss the habit you are helping her conquer and why, and stick to the consequences, no matter how much you'd rather shirk them.

> So lift your sagging arms. Strengthen your weak knees. "Make level paths for your feet to walk on." Then those who have trouble walking won't be disabled. Instead, they will be healed.
>
> Hebrews 12:12–13 NIrV

You can do this. Our children have trouble walking now ("No hands, no Jesus"), but let's not disable them permanently by coddling their poor choices or giving them the run of the house. May we give them a level, steady path to walk on in early childhood, and one day, by the grace of God, they will leave us healed and healthy—even holding hands and praying before dinner.

○ How would you describe your discipline? Is it working?

STEP OUT OF THE SPIN CYCLE

Resolve to set firm limits today. Enforcement is hard and inconvenient, but better now than in twenty years, when your children won't move out.

39

Lame Lineage

Over dinner recently, my girlfriends and I got on the topic of screwing up our kids. As their primary influence, it's basically inevitable. We went around the table predicting what our kids would one day say to their therapists:

"My mom was wound tighter than a ball of yarn."

"My mom loved cleaning more than her children."

"My mom screamed like a deranged monkey."

"My mom locked us in the backyard."

"My mom smacked me with a fairy princess wand."

"My mom fixated on parenting catchphrases she read in books."

"My mom once told me to dig my own grave."

Lord, have mercy. Our kids are going to have some issues to overcome. We can all predict the inevitable question posed to them: "So, let's talk about your mother. . . ." None of us are perfect, and all of us have failed.

But many of you have something more tragic to say about the home you were raised in. Things like:

"My mom was an alcoholic and looked the other way while my dad abused me."

"My dad left us."

"My mom's boyfriends made my childhood a living hell."

"My family was dirt poor and I often went hungry."

"My dad hit when he was angry."

"My parents were too busy to love me."

"I was always told I was a mistake."

You were crippled early by abuse, neglect, abandonment, or fear. You swore you'd never create a toxic home like the one you knew. You'd never drink. You'd never hit. You'd never leave. You'd assemble the family you never had.

Yet even so, maybe you struggle with the tendencies and habits that plagued your mom, your dad, your stepparent. Perhaps words have come out of your mouth that burned your ears as a child, or maybe stress reduces you to violence—it's what you know. You might see similarities rising up that scare the tarnation out of you.

A liar, a schemer, a victim, a prostitute, an adulterer, a murderer, a manipulator, an idolater, a rebel, a nobody . . . these were the members of Jesus's family tree. Girls, this is his heritage. He came from a long line of scoundrels and abusers. His ancestors were motley at best, scandalous at worst. And from this roll call of the troubled came the Savior of the Universe, the Star of Bethlehem, and the Rescue for Sinners.

Dear one, you are not bound to the failures of the generations before you. Their mistakes do not dictate your future, and liberation is yours through Jesus. I've seen countless women bravely break the cycle, raising children in a loving home when all they had known was violence. The abused do not have to abuse. The neglected can refuse to neglect. The injured can be an agent of healing through the redemption of Christ.

Jesus's mother said, "His mercy is upon generation after generation toward those who fear him" (Luke 1:50 NASB). Perhaps your parents didn't revere God, but you can become the first generation in this promise, a lightning rod for the mercy of heaven, a precursor for his grace on your children. There is no misery that Jesus cannot turn into ministry, no brokenness he cannot transform into beauty.

It is not your job to heal yourself; that is Jesus's work. This is his best area—you can trust him. He is a powerful healer. Your responsibility is to begin the hard work of forgiveness with Jesus. You can't break a destructive cycle when you're still chained to it by bitterness. Unforgiveness tethers you to a sinking ship.

In *Boundaries*, Henry Cloud and John Townsend wrote: "When you refuse to forgive someone, you still want something from that person, and even if it is revenge that you want, it *keeps you tied to him forever*. . . . [Forgiveness] ends your suffering, because it ends the wish for repayment that is never forthcoming and that makes your heart sick because your hope is deferred (Prov. 13:12). . . . Cut it loose, and you will be free."[8]

But don't mistake forgiveness for denial. God never denies an injustice. When we hurt him, he names it, he grieves it, he speaks his feelings about it. He doesn't declare it "okay" or "no big deal." Nor does he look the other way or brush it under the carpet. He deals with it, acknowledges his feelings, and then lets it go.

Forgiveness does not necessarily lead to reconciliation. God forgave the whole world of sin, but not everyone is in relationship with him. Why? They haven't owned their own sins yet. Forgiveness is one-sided. It has nothing to do with anyone being sorry. It happens in your heart when you release someone from the debt he owes you. You no longer condemn him. He is free from your anger.

And so are you.

Your entire lineage might be filled with scoundrels and deviants; your family history may resemble a tragic movie, like

---

8. Dr. Henry Cloud and Dr. John Townsend, *Boundaries* (Grand Rapids: Zondervan, 1992), 134–35. Emphasis mine.

Jesus's. But you've been rescued. You've been given the gift of motherhood. Your young children are innocent and pure; they are untainted by the baggage you were saddled with. You have a fresh slate to fill with love, laughter, mercy, and hope. Though you were injured, you will be a mender. Your old label might have been "unwanted daughter" or "abused daughter," but now it is "daughter of God," and nothing can remove that kind of honor. Jesus destroys the names that once defined us and replaces them with:

Beloved.

Redeemed.

Restored.

For the Mighty One has done great things for me; and holy is His name.

Luke 1:49 NASB

○ Are you a first generation Christ-follower? Welcome to the family. Do you still struggle with unforgiveness? Toward whom and why?

○ What are your dreams for your children and family?

STEP OUT OF THE SPIN CYCLE

One of the first steps toward forgiveness is empathy. Ask God to help you imagine what it was like for the person who hurt you when he or she was young. Try to put yourself in his or her shoes as a six year old.

40

Belovedness

John and Audrey are good friends of ours who pastor another church in our community. On the first day of school last year, we saw John walking his twins into kindergarten holding a long staff. "Are you planning to beat the children who badmouth your kids?" we asked in our classic sarcastic fashion. He laughed, then told us why he was carrying an oversized stick to Elm Grove Elementary.

The night before, John and Audrey held a commissioning ceremony where they spoke blessings over their children. For Tyler, they read the story of Moses. "Tyler, just like Moses, you are going to be a leader and God will never leave you. This is your staff that gives you courage and reminds you that God is faithful and nothing is impossible with him." Thus the staff. For Callie, they gave her the keepsake blankets given to the twins as babies and said, "Callie, you are like the 1 Thessalonians disciple, gentle among people like a mother caring for her babies. You will bring love and tenderness to the children you meet."

These precious parents spoke these powerful words over their children, commissioning them as disciples and commemorating their transition from home to school. They charged them with leadership and compassion, forever imprinting them with purpose. What marvelous parenting; we are so blessed to call them friends.

Girls, we have something special to offer our children beyond the physical care of their bodies. In Latin, the word "bless" is *benedicere*. The word "benediction" used in many churches means literally speaking (*diction*) well (*bene*). Mamas, we have the power to speak blessings into the lives of our kids. We can speak well of them, to them, and about them to Christ.

"According to Hebrew thought patterns," wrote Karla Worley, "the spoken word had a life of its own. It was not just an idea; it was a happening. When Isaac gave Jacob his blessing, rather than Esau, it was an act, a thing which had been done and could not be taken back. As well, the word, once spoken, had the power to fulfill itself. It could cause itself *to be*. To speak a blessing on someone was to cause them to be blessed."[9]

Henri Nouwen wrote, "[A blessing] is more than a word of praise or appreciation; it is more than pointing out someone's talents or good deeds; it is more than putting someone in the light. To give a blessing is to affirm, to say 'yes' to a person's Belovedness."[10]

Your children are beloved in so many ways. They are beautiful in spirit, adored by the Father. Who they are is wonderful—well beyond what they do. Their angels continuously see the face of God (see Matt. 18:10). Your children are innocent and trusting, hilarious and tender. Jesus loves them uniquely. They bring joy and laughter to our families. Their lives lie ahead of them, full of promise and potential.

We have the privilege to speak this truth into their lives, to call it forth. We can speak well every single day to our children: "You have a kind heart. Jesus loves that about you."

---

9. Karla Worley, *Traveling Together* (Birmingham, AL: New Hope Publishers, 2003), 151.

10. Henri Nouwen, *My Sister, My Brother: Life Together in Christ* (Ijamsville, MD: The Word Among Us Press, 2005), 99.

"God will never leave you. No matter what."
"God has so many special plans for your gifts."
"Let me show you this verse. It's for you."
"You are such an important part of this family."
"You make me so happy to be a mom."
"I love you."

Jesus said, "The words I have spoken to you are spirit and they are life" (John 6:63). Aren't they? Jesus has spoken life into millions of hearts. And we are called to imitate our Savior. We have life-giving power in the blessings we speak. When you tell me I am able in Christ, I am. When I tell my children they are beautiful in Jesus, they become more so. When we tell each other we are doing a wonderful job as mothers, we rise even higher to the occasion.

Let's call forth the blessedness in our children; we'll say "yes" to their belovedness. Let's speak words of power and mercy into their spirits, teaching them who they are in Christ from the littlest age. Speak the blessings of heaven into the raw material of who they are, which is the fiber of who they'll become: chosen, precious, loved, essential, gifted, redeemed, empowered, and cherished. These are true now, but they become even truer when we say them aloud.

Blessings are the greatest affirmation we can offer. Let's make sure our children are covered in them, just like Jesus did. "And he took the children in his arms, put his hands on them and blessed them" (Mark 10:16).

○ What blessedness can you call forth in your children? What is special about each one?

STEP OUT OF THE SPIN CYCLE

Tell them today. Speak blessings into their dear lives.

Jen Hatmaker has written eight books and Bible studies for women, including *A Modern Girl's Guide to Bible Study* and *Interrupted*. At least partial credit goes to her kids for supplying a steady stream of material: Gavin, twelve, Sydney, ten, and Caleb, eight. Jen has been happily married to her husband Brandon for sixteen years, and they live in Austin, Texas, where they planted Austin New Church. Adding a little more to the mayhem, they are adopting a child from Ethiopia, so the good material is sure to never run out. Jen speaks at conferences and retreats all over the nation. If you'd like her to come to your event, check her out at www.jen hatmaker.com.